Edward Bellamy, Solomon Schindler

Young West

A Sequel to Edward Bellamy's Celebrated Novel

Edward Bellamy, Solomon Schindler

Young West
A Sequel to Edward Bellamy's Celebrated Novel

ISBN/EAN: 9783337028503

Printed in Europe, USA, Canada, Australia, Japan

Cover: Foto ©Thomas Meinert / pixelio.de

More available books at **www.hansebooks.com**

Patent Applied for.

YOUNG WEST,

A SEQUEL TO

EDWARD BELLAMY'S CELEBRATED NOVEL

LOOKING BACKWARD.

BY

SOLOMON SCHINDLER.

BOSTON:
ARENA PUBLISHING COMPANY,
COPLEY SQUARE,
1894.

Arena Press.

YOUNG WEST.

CHAPTER I.

A nickname, once bestowed upon a man, clings to him forever. I am known as " Young West " all over the land, notwithstanding the fact that I am seventy years of age. My teachers and schoolmates used to call me " Young West." That was all very well at that period of life. If a person is to be distinctively qualified by the adjective " Young," childhood and youth are proper seasons for its application; but when people continued to call me " Young West " long after I reached manhood, it became aggravating. Is it not absurd that those who know me or of me still persist in calling me " Young West " even now that my hair has turned snow-white? I sometimes wonder if to crown the absurdity with an anti-climax, the words: " This is all that remained of Young West, who died in the year — at the age of seventy, eighty, ninety " (as the case may be), will be inscribed upon the urn containing my ashes.

I must confess that the nickname, though it was bestowed upon me good humoredly and was not suggestive of any trait of character, either good, bad, or indifferent, used to annoy me greatly, and particularly when persons, who were my juniors by many years, applied it to me. Perhaps I had grown more sensitive than was proper, but I can barely describe my mortification, when in the presidential campaign, which ultimately seated me upon the much coveted chair, the rallying cry was: "Young West against Mr. Blank." How I fumed and fretted when the papers printed paragraphs like the following: "The guild of textile-makers have declared for Young West;" or, The iron-workers are combining with the Electricians against "Young West" to offset the machinations of the grangers and cattle-raisers, who are pledged to elect "Young West." And mind, I was then in the fifty-seventh year of my life. I would have cheerfully foregone the honor for which I had been striving since I entered the industrial army as a private, if I could only have obliterated by my resignation the mortifying nickname "Young West;" — but no, "Young West" I have ever been, and "Young West," I am fated to die.

Looking upon this matter from the other side,

I must concede that the people, who are calling me " Young West," have some valid excuses for applying that sobriquet. Although I retired from public work many years ago, my physical constitution is yet sufficiently strong to stand the wear and tear, the worries and tribulations of any public office. Neither has my mind lost a particle of its former youthful freshness and vigor. My ideas are those of a young man. Old age has not made me a conservative, as it usually does of men.

In so far my friends are right, I am still *"Young* West."

My life has been crowded with memorable events ; good fortune permitted me to contribute somewhat to the welfare and progress of the nation, whom I served for a period of more than forty years. I ran through the whole scale of social and public ambition, from the lowest to the highest note. From one public office, I was promoted to the next higher one. Lifted and carried by the good will which my fellow workers bore me, I continued to rise until they intrusted me with the highest office in their gift, — the presidency. Even after I returned to private life, as prescribed by law, my advice and counsel was frequently solicited by my successors.

No wonder, therefore, my friends importune me now, as my days are fast ebbing away, to commit to writing the reminiscences of so eventful and so successful a career as has been mine.

Not that future historians would lack the material out of which to compose a thrilling biography of ex-president Julian West,— (or "Young West" as they most likely will call me)— for my name is attached to a multitude of documents of greater or less importance ; but my friends claim, that I am better qualified to explain the causes of events than my biographers ever will be. Their statements, they say, will be the product of research or hearsay, while mine will have the color and conclusiveness of personal observation. Who, moreover, could understand better than myself, how to sift the vast material, so as to select from it the most important and significant events, events that indeed determined the welfare of millions of people ?

That I yielded to those flattering exhortations, — or let me rather speak the truth — that I yielded to the promptings of my own vanity, the book, in the hands of the reader, sufficiently evidences. Why should I, after all, dissemble and deny, that to write this volume gave me intense pleasure ? Living over the incidents which I deemed worthy of preservation, I was thrilled a second time by the passions and impulses which then stirred me into action. Life is, indeed, twice enjoyed by man : once when it stretches out before him in the form of hopes and expectations ; the second time when he is reviewing it and beholds the accomplished facts, the real history of his being, ineffaceably preserved under the transparent crystal cover of the past.

It has been often said, and well said, that a man's life does not begin with the hour of his birth, not even with the moment of conception, that begins the life of the embryo, but that every existence is linked to previous ones by a long line of ancestors. Most of our good and evil traits, health as well as disease, we inherit from persons who have lived long before us ; to ignore the influence, which even our remotest ancestors have upon our being, would be like ignoring the rivulets and tributaries that form a river.

Biographers, therefore, always mention one preceding generation at least, that is, the parentage of the hero of their tale ; thus I, too, must make mention, before speaking of myself, of the nearest links that connect me with the past, of my father and mother. In the few lines which I feel bound to devote to them, the reader will find an additional explanation, how it happened that the nickname "Young West" was fastened upon me.

In the year 2001, the inhabitants of Atlantis (a city which occurs in the annals of mediæval history under the name of Boston), were thrown into a state or unusual excitement, which soon spread all over the inhabited world, when telegraphic and telephonic communication distributed the news.

Workingmen, while excavating a lot for building purposes, had struck upon a piece of antique architecture, upon a subterranean room, so admirably constructed that it had withstood the ravages of time for more than a century. The appointments of this room were rather strange. Air seemed to have been led into it by way of tubes, and light by way of electrical contrivances, which at once indicated the time when the chamber was built, as being that of the last decades of the 19th century. The furniture, which was found in the apartment, strengthened this conclusion; it coincided with the fashion plates of that period.

The discovery of this ancient structure would have received only a short mention in the "National News Register" had it not become intensified by a much more startling incident. The room contained also the body of a man ; not the skeleton of a man, nor his embalmed corpse,— the body that was found was that of a man, fast asleep.

All evidences indicated that this person had gone to sleep more than a century ago. The usual methods to awake a sleeper, failing, the most eminent physicians were convened and the extraordinary case was placed in their hands. One of them, Dr. Leete, had retired from practice many years ago. He had been paying of late, during his leisure, considerable attention to the medical inventions and discoveries of the nineteenth century, making a thorough study of Mesmerism or Hypnotism, as it was then called. He had read of a method by which such a sleep could be terminated ; he began to experiment and his endeavors were crowned with success; the sleeper opened his eyes.

The patient was now given entirely into his care. He removed him to his own apartment and by degrees he brought him to consciousness. He supplied carefully the organism of his patient with the most needed food and after a few days of cautious treatment, he dared open a conversation with his guest, disclosing to him little by little where he was.

The doctor's diagnosis of the case had been correct. Julian West, a wealthy resident of Boston, had been suffering for years from insomnia. Sleep fled from him even in his quiet underground apartment, which he had caused to be specially constructed for his use as a bed-chamber. When slumber would not come to him for many days and nights, he used to send for his physician who would apply the hypnotic process to put him to sleep. One of his body attendants, who had been instructed how to reverse the process, would wake him the next morning.

Mr. West could not tell or even imagine, why he had not been roused as usual the next morning, nor what had become of the house of which the discovered apartment was merely the subcellar. The only possible explanation, that he could think of, was, that perhaps the house had caught fire during the night and that his friends supposed him to have perished in the flames. Why the place was never utilized afterwards as a site for new buildings or why excavations were never made before on the same place, he was as unable to surmise as were the people who had found him.

The young man,— he appeared not older than thirty-five years,— became pitiably distracted, and for some time he was in danger of losing his reason. Thanks to the good care that Dr. Leete took of him, his mental equilibrium was quickly restored. As soon as he began to rally, he plied his host with questions of all kinds.

Since the time that he had gone to sleep, all social conditions had changed in such a marvellous manner that he failed to understand them. His age had been one of intense competitive strife, now he beheld society forming a brotherhood indeed, in which all worked for one and one for all. He could not understand how money should have ceased to be the stimulus for all individual efforts; he wondered that people were found willing to work without being paid for their labor; he could not see how it was possible that all could live in affluence, nor could he grasp the idea of economic equality. After a short time, however, he became not alone reconciled to our social arrangements, but he began to acknowledge their superiority over the conditions that prevailed in his time. He now wondered that his contemporaries could have been so blind as not to see the true remedy that would have cured all the evils of which they complained so much. He remembered now that at his time already some such ideas of

economic equality had been troubling the minds
of a few individuals and how the socialists,—
so these people had been called,— were scorned
and ridiculed as visionaries, yea, even persecuted
as enemies of society.

After his full recovery, he was given the position of professor of mediæval history in one of
our colleges. His specialty was to lecture on
the social conditions of the 19th century.
Speaking from his own experiences, his dis-
courses were very interesting and attracted wide·
spread attention.

The first woman whom his eyes met after
waking up from his protracted slumber, was the
daughter of his host. She was by occupation a
hospital nurse and had been detailed to take
special care of him under her father's directions.
It was, therefore, not astonishing at all that he
should have learned to love her, but that Miss
Leete should have reciprocated the feelings of a
person, who in fact was more than a hundred
years older than she was, and who,—as was
found out later on,— had been affianced to her
own great grandmother, was a surprise to all,
especially as she had not lacked suitors and had
been courted by young men of high promise.
So far, she had refused all offers of marriage,
reserving her hand,— so she said,— for one who

would distinguish himself by some great public deed. However, the fancies of women have always been and will forever be unfathomable; she returned Julian West's affection, and after a time they were registered as a married couple.

Their marital bliss was destined to be only of short duration. Julian had been restored to life and apparent health; still outraged nature took her revenge in due time. His tissues failed to procreate cells in sufficient numbers and of sufficient quality. He visibly fell off; he grew weaker and weaker, and finally he died, after a short illness, of exhausted vitality,—as the physicians termed it,—in the second year of his married life.

At the time of his death, his widow was expecting to become a mother, and when, two months later, she gave birth to a weak, sickly-looking boy, the medical authorities debated upon the possibility of such a child, ever developing into manhood.

Some physicians prophesied that, lacking the proper stamina, the first attack of measles, would remove "Young West," other doctors gave him a longer lease of life but predicted that phthisis would carry him off; but all agreed that "Young West" would never reach man's estate; that, should he live, he would never become a useful member of society.

Did their predictions come true? No. They were all disappointed. "Young West" grew up healthy in body and mind and lived to serve his country well. He had entered life — to speak in the language of the 19th century — well advertised, and it was perhaps due to that very notoriety that he succeeded where others failed.

CHAPTER II.

When the human soul enters life, the whole world forces itself, so to say, throws itself upon it at once, craving recognition. It would crush the new citizen by its pressure had not a wise Providence so ordained it that it can reach him only through one channel at a time, until he has accustomed himself to his environments and has become capable of bearing the world's full weight.

The tablets of memory, — white and clean at birth, — become soon covered with the marks inscribed upon them by passing events and although nobody can tell how many such impressions the memory received before it learns to bring them into order and to recall them at will, it is within the bounds of reason to assume that the infant receives through the senses, and stores away for future use, thousands of impressions every day.

The real awakening of the mind, however, occurs at a much later period, which varies as individual cases vary. Some will awake to consciousness as early as the second year, others not before the end of the fourth. In normal existences, the day or event can be fixed, when, for the first time, we remember ourselves either observing or acting. That day opens, in fact, the history of a man's life.

I awoke to consciousness not before I was three years of age, but I remember that moment distinctly. I found myself in the company of quite a number of children like myself. We had been playing upon the green turf in a garden, and a bell was calling us to lunch. — I hear the tolling of that bell yet. — I clearly remember that not only did I understand the meaning of that bell, but I also knew that, when hearing it, I was to take a certain place in a file to be formed by us children. Whether I had been trained before to act in that manner, — most probably I had, — I cannot remember. I only know that I took hold of the hand of another child, we placed ourselves behind several others and kept step to the music which was rendered by an orchestrion. I then remember that I tripped over some impediment and fell, dragging my companion with me. Both of us began to cry, upon which a pretty woman of about twenty-five years came to us, lifted us up, put us again on our feet, straightened our frocks and tiers, kissed us tenderly and said in a sweet, sympathetic tone : " Don't cry, dears, don't mind a tumble or a fall ; say ' hey ho' and let us run for lunch." With tears yet trickling from our eyes, we exclaimed : " Hey ho," and led by her we trundled into a spacious hall, where we took seats upon little stools at a long, low table. The scene appears before me as if it had occurred but yesterday. I recollect how we were regaled with milk, bread, and sweet fruit. I also remember the names of my playmates and the names of most of the women who attended to us. Miss Bella, who had special charge of me and a few others, and at whose hand I had entered the dining-hall, tied a napkin around me and supplied me with the food I seemed to need. How she knew, I could not tell at that time, but she knew exactly how much it was well for each of us to eat. To the one she would give a larger portion than to the other, and not rarely would she offer a diet different from that of the rest, to one or the other of the children.

After lunch, we went again into the garden. Some of us would play, others would lie down in hammocks and sleep. I remember that I liked all the nurses whom I met daily, but that I was most attracted by Miss Bella.

Every morning an elderly man would appear amongst us before whom we passed in file. Mr. Rogers — so we called him — was always received by us with pleasure. He would stroke our hair or kiss us. Sometimes he would play with us, make us catch him, roll with us on the ground and teach us games. He was usually accompanied by another man, whom we did not like as well, because he would make us open our mouths to put a little ivory stick right into our throats, a proceeding which we did not fancy very much. He would also take hold of the wrist of some child and do many more things which we children did not comprehend. We used to call him Uncle Doctor.

One of his actions remained a wonder to me until I learned its meaning. I will, therefore, give a true account of it, as it appeared to me at that time.

Some of the children seemed to be unwilling

to do what the nurses bade them do. They would strike and scratch other children, take away their toys or destroy without reason the flowers in the garden, or they would torment the rabbits, birds, or other animals which were kept therein. No matter how often the nurses would tell them that it was wrong to commit such deeds, these refractory children would not listen, but repeated the offence as often as they found a chance. Others were in the habit of not telling the truth. It seemed as if a certain impulse, over which they had no control, would drive them to do what was forbidden, or that it would give them a secret pleasure to commit deeds which would cause pain to others. Whenever one of us was hurt through the malice of such a young ruffian, our nurses would tell us not to retaliate and still to love him, because, they said, he was sick and would soon recover and then not do it again.

There was one dark-complexioned little fellow, a year older than myself, whom we called "Bobby," who seemed to derive special pleasure from annoying me. No sooner had Miss Bella turned her back to us than he would jump at me, scratch or pinch me or pull my hair. One day, he even threw a stone at me; it struck me on the head and I began to scream. Other children had seen him send the missile, but he still stoutly denied the deed.

" Don't mind it, Julian, dear," said Miss Bella, while dressing the wound, " Bob is a very sick boy, only sick children will throw stones at others."

The next morning, when Mr. Rogers, accompanied by " Uncle Doctor " entered our ward, I observed Miss Bella earnestly talking to them. They cast glances at me and also at Bob. When his turn came to be examined, the doctor took him kindly in his lap, talked cheerfully and pleasantly to him, as if nothing had happened and even made him ride upon his knee. Bob enjoyed the fun and clapped his hands in high glee. All at once the doctor made him recline on his arm, looked fixedly at him and said : " Poor Bobby is so sleepy, his little eyes feel so tired, his little legs are so weary ; Bobby is now closing his eyes, now he is going to *sleep !* "

The last word he intuned with a commanding inflection.

To my great surprise, Bob had indeed closed his eyes and was fast asleep.

The Doctor then began to talk to him softly : " Bobby will not wake until I count three ; Bobby does not want to pinch and scratch other children, Bobby will never throw stones **again**, do you hear me, Bobby?" Though his eyes were closed, Bobby said: "Yes sir."

The doctor continued: "Bobby will never again tell a lie, Bobby will go to Young West, kiss him and beg his pardon. One, two, three."

Bob opened his eyes. The doctor kissed him and put him on the ground.

I expected that Bob would come to me and do as he was ordered, but he did not. All that day, he was quiet and abstained from playing his usual tricks on me. The following day, the doctor held a similar conversation with him and again the next day. On the fourth day, to my surprise, Bob came to me and begged my pardon. For a few more days, the doctor seemed to be extremely friendly towards Bob without, however, putting him to sleep. After that, he took no more special notice of him than he did of the others.

Bob and I became fast friends after that. Perhaps because my attention had been drawn through Bob's case, I happened to see the doctor treat other children precisely in the same manner. When I questioned Miss Bella, whether Bob was yet sick, she answered: "No, he is just as well as the rest of you;—the doctor has cured him."

The nursery — for such was the place in which I came to consciousness — was attached to a block of residences quite in the heart of the city. It formed the southern wing of the square and was built like the houses, entirely of aluminum and glass. In the rear, the garden extended to which I have referred above, to be used as a playground. It was walled in by panels of glass and covered by a glass roof that could be opened and shut at short notice, so that we could stay in the garden even when the weather was not pleasant. In front of the nursery, was a kind of park, much larger than our garden in which the grown-up resi-dents of the block and their friends, would walk. We could see them and they could see us, but unless they entered the nursery by a side en-trance, communication was impossible. At all times of the day, persons could be seen in the park, who, in their turn would watch us at play or at our meals, through the windows. They would smile at us, and we would throw kisses to them.

The upper story of the building, to which we ascended by a broad staircase, was our dormi-tory. Each of us found there his little bed and his dressing case. In the cellar, to which light was carried through glass plates from above, was the lavatory, furnished with wash bowls and bath-tubs. Its most remarkable feature was a large tank that could be filled within a short time with lukewarm water. Dressed in our bathing suits, all of us — we numbered about a hundred — would plunge into it every morning with our nurses and such fun it was! The smaller ones would receive merely a good washing but the bigger ones were shown how to swim. I learned how to swim almost by myself and became quite an expert.

The routine of the nursery was about the same as it is in every nursery to-day. At seven o'clock in the morning, a bell warned us to rise. We slipped on our bathing robes and took our bath. After the nurses had dressed us, we partook of a light breakfast, consisting of milk, cake and fruit, as the season of the year permitted. After breakfast, with the exception of cold days, we were sent into the garden where the nurses employed our time with all kinds of instructive games. We would mould figures of clay or play in the sand or sow seeds in garden beds and watch them grow, or braid strips of paper into handsome patterns, or string beads, etc. Our little fingers were made nimble by all kinds of work. Before we got tired of one occupation, the head nurse would propose some other. She would teach us songs, tell us stories or show us pretty pictures. Thus the time passed unnoticed by us. Lunch time was welcome and after eating most of us would take a short nap. Refreshed by the sleep, we would spend the afternoon in games that tended to develop our muscles, or we would look into the park, watch the fountains play and listen to the concerts which were given there every afternoon. We learned to love music; we would file in and out of the halls to the strains of music, which an orchestrion supplied, and we would sing while marching; even during our meals, soft music was frequently rendered. At four o'clock we had dinner, which consisted of various courses of wholesome vegetable diet. Meats were not given to us; not before a child had reached his fourteenth year, was he allowed to taste either meat or fish. Dinner finished, we were apparently left to our own devices. We played what we pleased and with whom we pleased. Even if we were ever so noisy in the garden or in the play-rooms, we were not reprimanded. Mr. Rogers, who would invariably return at that hour and remain with us during the rest of the evening, would then watch our every action. As I found out afterwards, his eye discerned during these hours the talents and vices that were slumbering in every child; the talents he gave instructions for properly developing; the vicious inclinations, he ordered to be eradicated.

During these hours, we received also visitors. Men and women — the latter in larger numbers,— would come and stay and talk with us for a short time. Some would pick out a particular child and kiss and hug it. Why? I could not tell. Some came expressly to see me and frequently I heard people ask the attendant to show them " Young West." One lady, especially, paid me a visit once every week. As a rule, she came alone, only at times either a young man or an aged gentleman accompanied her. She would take me on her lap, inquire after my health, and she never left me without kissing me good bye. I liked her, but not any better than I did other ladies and not as much as I liked the nurses and in particular, Miss Bella.

Miss Bella once told me that the lady was my mother, the young man, her husband, and the old gentleman, who wore a blue ribbon in his buttonhole, her father, and consequently my grandfather. What that meant, I could not comprehend at that time, and when I asked her to explain, she said evasively : " Some day, you will know."

Also boys and girls, much older than we were, would occasionally call. Both Miss Bella and Mr. Rogers knew a great many of them. They had been brought up in the same nursery, but now, they were at school. They wore uniforms. I remember a boy coming expressly to show Mr. Rogers the silver cord which he wore for the first time around the collar of his uniform. He was so proud of it.

"What was school? Where was it? Was it a pretty place?"

Every year towards spring, a few of the older boys and girls left the nursery; they went to school. Their nurses kissed them good bye and cried when Mr. Rogers led them away.

Why did they shed tears?

After a few weeks, some of these children would return during visiting hours, dressed in their handsome uniforms. We were glad to see them, but they were rather haughty towards us. They would not join our plays and seemed always afraid that we might soil their jackets with our fingers. They said the school was very pretty and that they loved it much better than the nursery.

"Would the time ever come when I would be sent to school?" I asked Miss Bella. "Of course, you will," said she, "but don't think of

that now, my dear." Then she took me on her
lap and told me the pretty story of a little fir
tree who cared not for the pretty clouds that
passed over him, nor for the songs of the little
birds that had built their nests near by in the
branches of the bigger trees, nor for the gam-
bols of the rabbits that played near him in the
grass, because he yearned so much to go where
the other big trees went, which the wood-cut-
ters cut down every year and carried away on
heavy wagons. He would ask the clouds, but
they could not tell him what became of them.
They thought they had seen some of them far,
far away, floating upon the water, decorated
with many colored ribbons. Would he float
some day upon the water? He would ask the
birds and one of them told him that they had
once seen a little tree, like him in size, planted
in a warm room, holding candles and nuts of
gold on its branches. Would he ever enjoy
such a glory? Thus Miss Bella would finish
Anderson's pretty story, advising me to be
happy now and not to worry about to-morrow
or about " school."

About seven o'clock, a light supper was
served, after which we were put to bed.

In this pleasant manner, our days passed by.
The only discomfort that could befall us was

sickness. We all dreaded to be sick; not that we were not as well cared for as we were in the nursery, but because we had to go to the hospital, where we missed our usual companions. I remember that once, having fallen sick, I was sent to the hospital. An excellent nurse, the very personification of kindness and patience, took charge of me, but I felt lonesome because neither my playmates nor Miss Bella were allowed to come to see me, not even Mr Rogers. The only face known to me was that of " Uncle Doctor." Why was he allowed to visit places which the rest were not allowed to enter?

One lovely day in spring, when I was about six years old, Mr. Rogers told Miss Bella to prepare me and a number of other children for "school." While she was dressing me in my best cloth, she whispered into my ear: " To-day you will be sent to school; my darling has grown to be a big boy, you will soon forget Miss Bella. I assured her I would never forget her, but all the time I was burning with impatience to enter, what I imagined a still happier place, " school." How I yearned to wear a uniform with shining buttons! I would soon return, if for no other reason, than to show my new clothes.

Mr. Rogers led us out of the house. For the

first time in my life, I walked in the streets. I was surprised that there were so many people and houses. How large the world was!

We walked for quite a while, strange objects meeting our inquisitive eyes at every turn, when we reached a peculiarly constructed house. Mr. Rogers showed a paper to a man who was sitting behind an open window. " Another lot ? " said he, with an interrogative inflection ? " Strapping little fellows ! theirs is the future !

" This is " Young West," remarked Mr. Rogers. "In spite of the prediction of the doctors, I have developed him and I feel sure that he will live to be an old man."

" Young West ! " exclaimed the man, " you don't say ! Let me have a look at him."

Mr. Rogers took me upon his arm, so that the man in the window could see.

" The very image of his father," said the stranger, " what an excitement it was when he was found ! "

We descended a flight of stairs into a cellar ; a bell was heard and Mr. Rogers guided his flock of little ones into what appeared to us a little house. We took seats on benches ; a man closed the door behind us. The room, which was lit by electric lamps, began now to vibrate in a strange manner. About ten minutes might have passed, when the vibration ceased; a man opened the door, exclaimed some words, which I did not understand, and Mr. Rogers told us to follow him. We ascended a flight of stairs, passed through a building similar to the one in which Mr. Rogers had held a conversation with the man, who had known my father, and——

I had never seen the like before. There was a garden spreading before us a thousand times larger than the one in which we had been brought up. There were hundreds of trees and shrubs and flowers in full bloom. I had seen pictures of horses and goats and sheep, here I saw these animals alive, grazing in the pasture. In the centre of this ravishing paradise, stood a house, a palace, I should rather say. It was the "school."

Mr. Rogers announced our arrival by pressing a button. We heard the sound of a bell and the gate of the palace flew open.

We entered.

CHAPTER III.

At the time when our present order of society had been in its first stages of conception, its friends and advocates believed, that it would tend to break up their colossal cities and would spread the inhabitants more evenly over the land. Their predictions never came true. The cities, instead of diminishing in size, grew to still larger proportions. The methods of agriculture, of manufacture, of locomotion, of distribution, had been improved in an undreamed of manner, so that people could combine with ease the pleasures of city life with the various occupations that required their presence elsewhere.

Travelling at the rate of more than one hundred and fifty miles an hour, people could cultivate the land in a radius of three hundred miles, or do their work in factories, scattered in such a circle, and still live in a city, leaving their homes in the morning and returning in the afternoon.

Although steam had long ago been replaced by electricity, and the smoke that hovered over mediæval cities, no longer vitiated the atmosphere, and although the improvements in regard to the sanitation of cities, had made them healthier abodes than they were in former centuries, still the concentration of millions of people within a comparatively small compass could not but produce a number of unavoidable disadvantages, among which the noise caused by the locomotion of so many people and the exhalations rising from so many bodies, were the least.

For more than half a century, the authorities had been wrestling with the question, where the public schools could be placed best, so that the children might obtain the polish which urbanity gives, without incurring the dangers unavoidably connected with city life. At last, a solution was found. It was, as is usually the case, so simple that they wondered why they had not thought of it before. They removed the schools out of the crowded districts into the suburbs; not too far, so as to preclude easy communication with the city, and yet sufficiently distant, so as to give to the children purer air, an abundance of light, plenty of elbow room for sports and that quietude which is needed for successful studies.

The many sights and the noises of city life had eaten away the nerve-force of the children of former generations. Nervous prostration had been a common disease among the dwellers of

great cities in the 19th century. The schools
had weakened the eyesight of pupils and every
third person in the street wore eye-glasses.
Rounded, stooping shoulders were then the distinguishing mark of the scholar. These mistakes
of the past were to be avoided. People came to
see, that next to life, the child was entitled to
the possession of a healthy body. A strong,
healthy soul was sure to develop therein.

Every large city is now encircled by magnificent school buildings ; the most beauteous sites
are selected for them and no labor or expense is
spared to make them efficient and effective to
do their work well and to rear citizens, well
equipped, both physically and mentally, to assure
the continuity of a prosperous and happy society.

The school to which our little troop was assigned, was one, which in the language of my
father's century would have been called a " Primary " school. It was built to hold about one
thousand children of both sexes, of ages ranging
from six to ten years. At my time, the number
of inmates was about nine hundred, not counting
the teachers and the staff of officials.

The building, like all our modern buildings,
was constructed of aluminum and glass. Pillars,
beams, spars, partitions, floors, doors, stairs,
were all made of aluminum, the walls of plain

white, or stained glass, according to location. The building was covered by a huge cupola that could be opened and closed at will, permitting excellent ventilation. The whole structure formed a large square.

The building contained on its first floor the offices of the various overseers, several reception rooms and a library. The second and third floor contained apartments for the teachers. The first floor of the right and the left wing was divided into class-rooms, the second floor contained dining halls and kitchens, and the third floor dormitories; the boys occupying the northern and the girls the southern wing. In the building in the rear on an underground floor were situated the natatorium, lavatory and the usual sanitary arrangements; on its first floor a gymnasium and on its second floor, workshops of all kinds for manual training. The third floor formed a large amphitheatre to be used for exhibitions, concerts, theatrical performances, etc. At some distance from the square, were located a hospital, the stables, in which all kinds of domestic animals were kept, and a poultry yard.

The electricity for heating, lighting, and cooking purposes, as well as for running the various machines of the house was received by way of underground wires from the city. We were

also connected by telephone with almost every
large place in the state. Some of the supplies
were sent to us from the national stores through
pneumatic tubes, others were raised in the
gardens which surrounded the school. The large
space between the four buildings, covered by the
dome, was used as a playground when the
weather was not pleasant.

Mr. Peters, the director of the school, received us in person. This day was one of the
most busy days of his scholastic year, because
almost every hour brought another troop of little
ones to his institution. He could not, therefore,
devote a great deal of attention to each company.

Mr. Rogers handed our records to him. Cast-
ing a quick glance over the list, Mr. Peters
chanced to see my name.

"Which of these children is Young West?"

Mr. Rogers pointed out my little person to
him. He looked at me searchingly, stroked my
hair, but made no further remarks.

He seemed to be a very kind man, yet I
began to feel sorry, that I was to part from
my former guardian; tears came in my eyes and
not until Mr. Rogers had promised that I would
soon receive permission to visit the nursery, did
I become consoled.

One of the teachers took us now to the

dining-hall and offered us refreshments. While we were yet seated at the table, a number of boys and girls, inmates of the school, marched into the room with measured steps. They were members of the senior class and the present year was their last in the primary school. They were distinguished from the rest of the pupils by a silver cord fastened around the stiff collars of their jackets. They placed themselves behind us, and, after we had finished our meal, each of them took two of us by the hand and showed us all over the house. From that day, for a term of a whole year, the little mentors assigned to us, were held responsible for our comfort.

Of the lowest grade, i. e., of the recruits, two only were assigned to one senior. Of the second grade, one senior had charge of five, and of the third grade, over ten. This was a wise arrangement because the smaller a child is and the less used to the rules and discipline of the school, the more attention does he require. To look after two such little ones, was all that could be expected of a child of nine years. After one or two years' experience, when we knew what was wanted of us, a member of the senior class could overlook, with ease, five, or even ten.

Children, to be sure, become more easily

attached to other children than to grown-up persons. They understand them much better and are less afraid of them. Within half an hour, I had closed a covenant of everlasting friendship with the boy into whose care I was given; so had Harry, my companion.

Our little mentor took us to the dormitory, showed us our clothes-press, assisted us in undressing and helped us to put on our new uniforms. He rolled our former wearing apparel into a bundle which was to be returned to the nursery. This day, being a holiday, he took us during the rest of it to the playgrounds, into the gardens, to the hennery and to the stables. We were all ears and eyes; Milton Green, that was his name, never tired of our questions. He seemed to be proud of his new office, glad to be of use to us, and to show how much more he knew than we little ones.

In our wanderings, we fell in with some boys and girls of the second grade, whom we had known in our nursery, among them, Bob, who joyfully exclaimed: "Why, there is Young West! I'm so glad to see you in school!"

He inquired after Miss Bella and the rest of our mutual friends. From that moment, Milton Green, and with him all my new companions began to call me "Young West." "Young

West, you are wanted in the office," or, " Young
West, let us have a run," or, " Young West,
make haste, lest you will be late for dinner."

Children are quick and keen observers;
when, therefore, my companions observed that
the teachers seemed to bestow some additional
attention upon me, they, too, sought my companionship. After a few weeks, " Young West "
was a favorite with all.

*　　*　　*　　*　　*　　*　　*　　*

Eight hours sleep, eight hours work, eight
hours recreation is the general rule observed in
all our institutions. At our school, it was
adhered to in its spirit rather than its letter.
No objections were ever raised, if children,
whose constitutions required more sleep than
eight hours, would use some of their leisure
time to take a nap. Neither were labor and
recreation divided by hard and fast lines.
Some of our labors were quite a recreation to
us, while during the hours set aside for recreation, we would sometimes engage in work,
which, though playful, demanded a larger expenditure of muscular or brain force than
actual labor did.

There was another rule to which we were
held. Whatever useful work children of our
age could perform, we were expected to do.

Thus we learned not to depend upon the services of others for our personal comfort, while on the other hand, we were instructed never to refuse friendly aid to the ones who were in need of assistance. Our little mentors, or our teachers, would show us how to perform a task well, but we, ourselves, had to do the work in every case.

A great many changes have occurred since I was a boy and many valuable improvements have been introduced; however, it is a delight to me to remember my school days and it gives me pleasure to pass in thought again through the routine of one of them.

From the dome of the building was suspended a large dial of a clock. It was regulated by electricity from the provincial timepiece and a gong connected with it would strike automatically all quarters, half hours, and hours. At six o'clock in the morning it would set free our orchestrion, and thus music would wake us from sleep and tell us that it was time to leave the bed.

This mode of rousing us from slumber had been introduced only a few years before I entered school. Before this, the sound of a bell would give the signal, but it was found that many of the little ones did not hear it. The frequent striking of the clock as well as the many signals that were given during the day by means of bells, had accustomed their ears to these sounds so that they failed to rouse them in the morning. The authorities, therefore, introduced music, not as a luxury but as a necessity. An officer would set every night the orchestrion for a new piece of music. The repertoire covered a whole year so that the selections should not become tiresome.

In summer, or when some pleasure trip was to be undertaken, we would rise before the official hour. Ordinarily, however, we all rose after the first few measures of the music were heard.

Our first work was to air our beds; this done, we hastened to the natatorium or the lavatories.

The natatorium could not accommodate all of us at a time, therefore, we took turns. Some would take their daily bath in the morning, others at noon, others before retiring at night. The ones, who did not bathe that day in the morning, washed, and combed their hair in the lavatories. Returning to the dormitory, we finished our toilet, and the beds, having been properly aired, were now made by us.

Who would have believed in ancient times

that children of six years could perform such labors? Of course their sleeping arrangements were so clumsy, that to keep them in good and healthy conditions was an unpleasant and tiresome work; but our light aluminum cribs, could be lifted with ease by two children. It took little strength to turn the air mattresses and cushions and after we had been shown three or four times how to spread sheets and blankets, we performed that task with neatness. Under the supervision of the mentors, two of us children would first make the one bed and then the other. Within five minutes all was done. Two of the larger boys then pressed down a lever which opened the upper window panes, and two others set free the fanning machine which in less than fifteen minutes purified the air.

To be tidy is but a habit. If a child is trained from his earliest youth to put everything in its proper place, and what is much more, if a proper place is prepared for everything, neatness becomes with him a habit. After a few weeks, none of us needed to be told how to keep his personal property in order; through mere force of habit, none of us would think of leaving a comb or towel on the floor or on the chair, or place an article where it did not belong.

Time was ours until 7.15 A. M., when we assembled in the dining-hall for breakfast. Around
every table, sixteen of us were seated, namely :
five mentors with their charges, making fifteen,
and an officer to supervise them. Fruit, milk,
and bread, were placed in plenty upon each
table, and we helped ourselves. We were allowed to talk and laugh at meal times, but not
so loud as to interfere with the comfort of others.
Embarrasing others or playing tricks upon
others for fun was avoided as shameful. It was
of rare occurrence that a pupil would overstep
the limits of propriety and would have to be
reprimanded.

The dining-halls extended over the second
floor of the two side wings but neither of them
was given to the exclusive use of either boys or
girls. We dined together, studied together, and
played together. Only our dormitories were
located in opposite wings of the house.

After breakfast, we would play for a while in
the yard or in the gardens, read, do some work
to which we had taken a fancy, or we would
watch the older boys at their rougher games.
At eight o'clock, we repaired to our class rooms.

To every subject of study, a full hour was
devoted, but no distinction was ever made as in
the schools of old, between geography and his-

tory, or between natural history and physical science, or between drawing and modelling, or reading and grammar, or writing and orthography; all related studies were combined into one. They were taught by expert teachers and in rooms fitted up for the purpose. Each class, when in full strength, numbered not more than twenty-five pupils. At the sound of the gong, each class would file into its class-rooms to be instructed by teachers who were masters in their branch. Very few books were used; the teacher imparted knowledge mainly by means of conversation. His aim was not so much to cram the head of the child with facts, as to develop his mind. Books were used only when labor was to be saved; when the art of reading and writing was to be practiced, or when tasks in arithmetic were given to the whole class. On the other hand, no object was ever discussed in a class without placing it, or a good model or illustration of it, before the pupils. Thus we always knew what we were talking about and, moreover, acquired the habit of observation.

Our school government took great pride in these methods of instruction which preserved the eyesight of the pupil, and not infrequently were we informed that in ages long past by, eyeglasses had been a badge of scholarship. " Young

West's own father," one of our teachers once
told the class, "could not read a line without
the use of spectacles." Then he produced photo-
graphs of men of the 19th century who were
renowned for their scholarship and lo, and behold. most of them wore eye-glasses. Some had
them tied to a string or chain, others had them
set in a frame.

After every hour of mental work, we either
had a half hour's lesson in gymnastics or calisthenics or an hour's lesson in manual work.

Dinner was served at 12 M. It consisted of
delicious vegetable soups, eggs, cakes, bread and
fruit. The bill of fare was changed each day.
On Sunday and Wednesday, delicacies were
more numerous than on the other days of the
week.

Till two o'clock, we were free to employ our
time as we chose. Instructions then followed
until 4 P. M. The hours from four to six were
again our own. During that time visitors would
come to see us or we would take a walk in the
fields or amuse ourselves in the gymnasium, or
indulge in sports. Some classes would take
their turn in the natatorium.

At 6 P. M., the gong called us to supper which
was similar in kind to the other repasts. After
supper, one hour's time was devoted to house-

hold work preparatory to the next day. We would clean our clothes and shoes, sew on a button that threatened to fall off, darn a stocking or mend a rent. We learned how to do all such work, the older boys and girls helping the younger ones. As our fingers were made nimble through the handling of all kinds of tools, such work was more of a pleasure to us than a drudgery

In summer time, weather permitting, we would spend the hours from 8 to 10 in the gardens; in winter, we would play games indoors or listen to recitations, or concerts in the large hall, which were frequently given by delegations from neighboring higher schools, that came to visit us. Those who needed more hours of sleep were excused from attendance and could seek their beds whenever they felt tired. At 10 o'clock all retired for the night.

This routine was never broken except on Wednesdays, Sundays, and on national holidays. On these days, the class rooms were closed and the whole time was ours. We would then travel in groups to the city to see the sights and return calls, or make excursions into the country. It happened only in the first year that such privileges were denied to a few on account of misconduct; in the second year, hardly any--

one was found who would not cheerfully yield to order, and in the fourth year, a deserved reprimand, would have lost for the culprit his mentorship, a humiliation which in very rare cases was incurred or inflicted.

The fact that we were always under the eye of some one and that no deed could be perpetrated in secret, accounts for the rare occurrence of any action on our part that could be called bad. Some teacher was always observing us and no sooner were any evil tendencies in our characters discovered than they were uprooted either by moral instruction and rational expostulation, or in obdurate cases by the medical advisor who was attached to the official staff of every school.

The health in general was good. The hospital was rarely filled. Wise precautions made much physicking unnecessary. I cannot remember ever having been seriously laid up, except once, when in a race, I fell and fractured my collarbone. I was carefully bandaged, remained for a few days in the hospital, and then returned to my class.

A word in regard to our apparel. Our clothes were simple, durable, seasonable, and artfully designed and trimmed. In each school, the pupils wore clothes of a different shade. Ours

were of a light blue. In summer, we wore
white calico waists, knee trousers, made of light
woolens and a jacket of the same material. Our
shoes were made of soft leather that required
oiling once every week. Rubbing with a damp
cloth would keep them clean. A soft cap, trimmed like the jacket and trousers, with braid of
a darker shade, covered the head. Oxidized
silver buttons formed a kind of ornamentation.
Our underwear was made in part of silk and in
part of fine wool. For winter wear, the materi-
als were heavier, and an overcoat was added; so
wore leggings and rubber boots. The girls
were dressed almost like the boys; they wore
wide pantaloons covered by a short skirt. Each
child had three changes of underwear and two
sets of clothing. The boys were supplied in
addition with overalls and the girls with wide
tiers for use at the work-bench or at any kind
of work that was likely to soil their garments.

Speaking of cleanliness, it was easy, and it
gave us pleasure to observe it. Our teachers
told us how in former times people used to constantly war against dust and filth without ever
succeeding; how they became discouraged and
allowed disintegrating matter to accumulate;
how the work of cleaning was most unwillingly
performed and called a drudgery. But they

also informed us that our ancestors had to con-
tend with a great many difficulties that are
unknown to us. Our sanitary arrangements and
lavatories are of the best, and easily accessible;
our roads are well paved; smoke, cinders, and
ashes are unknown because electricity is used
now for all purposes for which formerly fires
had to be built; our buildings and furniture,
made of lacquered aluminum and glass, are
cleansed by delicately constructed machinery
that operates automatically. The very germs
of unclean matter are removed by the most
powerful of disinfectants, electrified water, that
is sprayed over our walls, and penetrates into
every crack and crevice. The uncleanliness of
the people of which the historians of former
ages complain so frequently, was caused partly
by their lack of machinery, partly by the moral
discouragement which is apt to seize upon men
when labor will never show satisfying results,
partly, also, by the unequal distribution of the
means of subsistence. Unclean matter, we
were taught, is one of the most persistent
enemies of humanity; it poisons the health and
destroys the lives of millions. It defies individual assaults and it yields only when attacked by
combined efforts.

CHAPTER IV.

The subjects which were comprised in the
course of our studies, were not made in themselves the end and aim of instruction, they were
used in our schools as means of developing cor-
responding mental or physical abilities. Mathe-
matics, for example, were taught not for the
sole purpose of making mathematicians of the
pupils, but rather for the purpose of exercising
and developing their logical faculties; geography and natural sciences were taught for
the purpose of imparting the habit of keen
observation ; drawing, to awaken their sense of
the beautiful ; language, to train them in the
proper expression of thought ; manual work to
practice eyes and hands ; gymnastics to develop
muscular force and general health. Our teachers cared less for the readiness and skill
acquired in a certain branch of knowledge, than
that the real end and aims were attained by its
study and its relation to the other branches.
Special abilities are, after all, gifts of nature.
The talented will grasp all in one lesson and

excel in it with scarcely any effort on their part. Persistent training, it is true, can accomplish much even with children who are not gifted, but whatever results are obtained, they are bought at a high price, by the suppression of some other, natural talent.

Our social order employs only the talented for every kind of work which is to be performed; thus we are obliged to try and discover these natural gifts and to develop them. A great many branches of study which had figured prominently upon the programmes of the schools of the nineteenth and twentieth centuries, are, therefore, entirely ignored by us.

We were taught in our primary school how to read, write and cipher, we were directed to observe all objects surrounding us; we were trained how to express our thoughts in proper language; and in addition, we learned how to draw, to model in clay, and to handle and use all kinds of tools.

The observant eye of our teacher easily detected the talents that slumbered in every child. Though we were told to take part in every kind of work in which the class was employed, we were never discouraged by vituperation if we failed in branches for which we showed no special aptitude, while we were encouraged by praise when we gave indications of the possession of special gifts.

After the first year, our teachers formed some estimate in regard to our natural talents and in the second they assigned us to classes in which courses were pursued that tended to develop these special aptitudes.

A boy, slow in figures, but quick in observation, was not retarded on account of his failure in arithmetic; he was placed into a class in which that branch took a secondary rank but in which full scope was given to observation. Whoever excelled in practical work was not discouraged or called a dunce because of his failure in purely mental work and vica versa.

I showed talents and a decided predilection for all kinds of manual labor. I was handy with tools and showed special aptitude for keeping my belongings scrupulously clean. My shoes had a superior gloss, my clothes never showed a stain, my bed-clothes were neatly folded. I was also a good draftsman, and I preferred to convey my thoughts by a drawing or a model rather than by verbal description. I delighted to assist in the housework, and to dig in the garden was a keen pleasure. I executed with neatness whatever task was given to me. I learned to read fluently and to write a legible hand, but I cared little for literature. I began to warm up for physical science only when we studied chemistry in later years. In figures, I was very slow, and only geometry and trigonometry had some charm for me. I displayed no rhetorical talents, and whatever successes I had in after life, were never the result of captivating speech. I could state a fact in plain language, but whenever I failed to convince by argument, I was utterly lost. I could reach the head but never the heart of a listener.

My second year found me in a class in which these, my natural talents were allowed a wider scope, and when I left school at the end of four years, I was assigned to a higher graded school in which the manual arts and labor received special attention and were given more time than studies of a literary nature.

I had been a tiny babe and a weakly child, now I began all of a sudden to grow and to develop. My chest expanded and my muscles hardened. I could run, jump, climb, row or swim for hours without fatigue. There were others of my size and age who were my superiors in these sports, but I did not stand very far below them in rank.

I acquired the knack of handling tools with

ease. In my last year, Mr. Peters frequently detailed " Young West " for work in the garden, and he used to watch with apparent. delight how I swung a little pick axe or plied a small sized spade.

My relations to my classmates were of a most pleasant nature. We formed one brotherhood; as there were no private interests that clashed with one another, there was never cause for discord. Some boys, of course, had attractions for each other stronger than had others for them, but indifference and even instinctive moral antipathy never was fanned into hostility by harsh conflict.

I associated a great deal with girls and with boys who were younger than myself. Little as I cared for literary pursuits, I admired literary attainments in others and could pass hours with boys and girls who excelled in mental studies but had no taste for manual labor. I felt a kind of superiority over them, when they sought my advice or came to ask my assistance. This preference developed by no means a dislike towards such of my friends, who displayed talents like mine. Quite to the contrary, we would depend upon one another's help, whenever we undertook a work that one could not well perform alone. We would then put our

heads together and plan and discuss and design
the task. Yet a most pleasurable feeling came
over me whenever I was sitting among some
younger boys or girls, listening to their
prattle, and saw them watching the development of a toy, that I was making for one of
them, under the clever treatment of my knife.

Our teachers loved us and we idolized them.
Every child found in one or the other his ideal,
but that was not so great a miracle, as it may
appear. Mr. Peters, constantly watchful of the
unfolding of our talents, assigned us judiciously
to the care of teachers who were specialists in
the very branches we loved so well. Thus it
was but natural that we should admire their
knowledge, and eagerly imbibe their instruction.

Besides, Mr. Peters, whom we all admired
and loved, and who seemed to be with us everywhere, and on all occasions, I thought a good
deal of two teachers. One was a woman and
the other a man.

Mrs. Howe was about thirty-five years of age.
She was the wife of one of our male teachers,
Mr. Howe. She had two children, a boy of
twelve years, who was a member of the school
for which we prepared, and a girl of nine years,
who was the inmate of a primary school like
ours. According to the laws, children of teach-

ers, had to receive their instruction elsewhere; they came, however, on visiting days to see their parents. Mrs. Howe, I think, loved some of us scarcely less than her own children; I was especially, one of her favorites. She taught us how to draw, how to model in clay, and similar work but while I was quick in these lessons and admired her artistic creations, I became much more attached to her for the fascination and sweetness of her personality. I loved to be in her company; and she had always a kiss or a kind word for me. I imagined she loved me better than the rest, although she seemed as kind and considerate to all. A flock of little ones would surround her whenever she crossed our playgrounds. From her I learned,— I have good cause to believe,— the neatness and accuracy in work, which in after life, helped me so much and raised me to the position of an officer in the industrial army.

Mr. Groce was a specialist in horticulture; he had charge over the extensive gardens that surrounded our school. A staff of helpers worked under his direction, but some of the gardening was done by us children. We worked slowly, it is true, but when fifty of us were ordered to dig a trench or to weed flower-beds, it took no more time than if two or three

men, even five, had been set to work at it.
And what pleasure it gave us to work in the
garden under Mr. Groce's eye! He would show
us how to hold our little spades and rakes to
best advantage. "Do your work with your
heads," he would say, "and you will not blister
your hands. Never go twice when you can
attain the same results by going once." He
was ever watchful that we did not overwork or
overheat ourselves. No matter how eager we
were sometimes to finish a task, he would make
us stop when he observed that our youthful
strength was getting exhausted. He disliked to
see work done in a slipshod manner. "Take
your time, boys and girls," he would say, "but
do your task properly."

Although fruit and vegetables formed the
larger part of our fare at the table, children love
to eat fruit that they pick themselves off the
trees and bushes. He never objected to our
picking berries or plucking cherries. He only
warned us not to waste useful food and not to
destroy our health by over indulgence. I cannot remember any boy or girl who ever ate
in the garden more than an occasional berry,
or a few cherries. Even in the fall, when
we helped to harvest the ripe fruit, we did
not think of either willfully destroying the

fruit or appropriating any for our own immedi-
ate appetites.

Mr. Groce seemed to take special interest in
me. "I see no reason why "Young West"
should not live to be an old man," he said, "he
is growing stronger every day and harrows and
digs like a little man." He himself was a lover
of athletic sports, an expert rider on the cycle;
an excellent swimmer and none of the teachers
in the school surpassed him in pitching ball.
Such qualities were sure to be admired by us
boys and as Mr. Groce would drop now and
then a hint to me how such feats could be
accomplished, it was quite natural that I loved
him and that he stands before me even now,
the very ideal of manliness.

When I speak of Mrs. Howe and the teachers
whom I loved best while attending the primary
school, I wish by no means to intimate that I
looked upon the rest of the teachers with coldness, indifference or dislike. They were all
well-trained educators, who had chosen their
occupation out of pure love for it and it would
have been a miracle had they not succeeded. I
singled out these two teachers, and clung to
them with particular love; but other schoolmates of mine displayed similar affection for
other teachers and felt for Mr. Groce and Mrs.

Howe no greater liking than I felt toward their favorites.

Besides the staff of instructors, some officials lived in the same building with us, who provided for our wants. There were cooks and bakers, engineers, carpenters, iron-workers, masons, cobblers, and butchers; there were gardeners and men who attended to the cattle, and the products of the farm and dairy. We children came frequently in contact with them; we delighted to watch them at work, and frequently some of us were asked to help them or do some light work under their direction.

I had many friends among them, especially among the men who took care of the animals. I enjoyed being near and around the stables in which all kinds of domestic animals were kept. Our cows supplied the hospital with fresh milk. The milk supply for the whole school came in a condensed form from the large national ranches where,—as we were told,— thousands of heads of cattle were kept.

The few horses supported in the stables, were used to cart farm products from the fields and gardens to the barns; for the transportation of persons, bicycles and electric carriages sufficed. A few sheep and goats were kept to serve as objects for our lessons, so were the inmates of

the poultry yard. The men and women, attending to the stables and farmyard never tired of
answering intelligently all our questions in
regard to the life and habits of the animals in
their charge. They showed us, how, when
kindly treated, these dumb creatures will
return our love by sincere devotion. If one of
us children showed an inclination to be cruel
to animals, he was treated as one suffering from
a mental disease. When I was laid up in the
hospital, with a broken collar-bone, I observed
that one of the boys was put to sleep and
spoken to by the doctor in the same manner as
I remembered my friend Bob once was treated
in the nursery.

In the midst of so large a number of children,
it happened that the ones who had the same
likings met more frequently and at the same
places, than did the rest; that they discussed
the subjects in which they were interested more
thoroughly and hence became more closely
attached to one another. Granting opportunities for thus grouping themselves in perfect
liberty, the teachers easily discovered the in-
born talents of their pupils. They formed
congenial classes of them and made their favorite topics the main objects of study. The
pupils thus learned with eagerness and grasped

a lesson in a very short time. Under this system of teaching, none needed to be stimulated, quite to the contrary, teachers had frequently to curb the eagerness of boys or girls who wished to proceed before they had fully mastered a previous lesson.

To teach pupils, who are eager to learn, is easy. The troubles which teachers of previous ages experienced, arose from the fact that they were forced to teach children who were unwilling and sometimes unable to learn certain lessons. I own a manuscript containing a number of lectures which my father prepared and delivered shortly before his death. In one of them, he describes his life in school. Teachers were at his time censured when a sufficient number of their pupils failed to pass an examination. They were obliged, therefore, to almost pump a lesson into a dull child's head. Dull? By no means. The children of that age were as bright as are ours, but they were forced to study things for which they had neither taste nor talent and were not permitted to select studies for which their innermost soul was yearning.

What happy days my school days were when compared with those of my father's time!

CHAPTER V.

Some time, of course passed by, before I had accustomed myself to my new surroundings. So many objects crowded upon my mind that my full attention was enlisted to master them. Time flew and more than four weeks had passed before I gave a thought to the nursery or the friends whom I had left behind. It was even by accident that I was reminded of them one day.

I happened to meet Mr. Rogers in our yard. Of course I ran to him; he took me up in his strong arms, kissed me tenderly and asked: "How is Young West? Why, you have grown to be quite a little man since I saw you last. How pretty you look in your uniform! but you seem to have forgotten us, you never came to call upon your old friends." I could hardly keep back my tears. "I have not had a chance," I stammered. Then I asked after Miss Bella and the rest, naming a string of children whom I knew. Mr. Rogers gave all the latest news from the nursery. Before parting, he promised that he would arrange for me to visit the nursery at an early day.

On the following Wednesday, Milton Green received orders to take his two wards into the city. He had made the trip at various occasions, but heretofore, he had been under the supervision of a guardian, this time he was to act independently and what was a much greater honor to him, he was to take charge of his two little wards.

The night previous to this, my first visit, I was very restless, and could not get to sleep. Long before the orchestrion began to play, I was wide awake, while Milton, whose bed stood at my right, slept as if the proposed excursion was an every day affair with him. I passed in my mind through all the pleasures which I expected on the holiday. We were not alone to visit the nursery but to see some other friends. We were to call at the place where my mother and grandfather lived, then at the residence of Milton's relations, finally, at the parents of Harry, our companion.

How slow the hands on the dial of the large clock moved! Would morning never dawn? For the first time, I heard the wheels in the orchestrion squeak, previous to the intonation of the musical piece — then came the blast of cornets and trombones, the clashing of cymbals, the roll of drums; at last — the boys opened dream-

more than two hundred children had received
permission to visit the city. Each mentor
received a number of cards. Some of them, I
observed, Milton showed at the tunnel stations,
others, he showed at the place where we took
lunch, one in the hippodrome, in which we were
told to spend the afternoon.

A few of our teachers took the same train
with us, but did not appear to supervise us; we
enjoyed perfect freedom. By way of the tunnel
route, we reached the city after a few minutes
ride.

One month ago, when I passed the streets
for the first time, the sights so bewildered me
that I observed almost nothing. Now all came
back so me. My friend Milton, in addition, felt
duty-bound to call our attention to every large
structure on our way and to explain its purposes.

The trees, which lined the streets, the parks
which intersected the squares, did not impress us

very much; there were larger trees near the school and the parks did not compare with our gardens. The buildings, the streets, and the people, that swarmed therein on foot, on bicycles, and in electric vehicles surprised us much more.

"This is the teachers' club-house," Milton would say, "Here teachers meet and have a good time." We saw, indeed, some of our teachers entering. "Here is the post office; here are the sample-rooms; and right here in the neighborhood is the supply department. I have never been inside of any of these buildings, but boys who have seen the interior, could not stop speaking of the pretty things they saw exhibited therein for sale. They are 'immense.'" Immense was a favorite word of Milton's. He would apply it indiscriminately to express surprise or admiration.

I had frequently observed some large objects flying through the air and Mr. Groce had told me that they were "aeroplanes." These air ships were moved by electricity and people would employ them when they travelled to foreign countries, particularly when they had to cross oceans. We now saw one of these machines starting from the top of a tower. The people upon it waved their handkerchiefs as they rose higher and higher, until they vanished out of our sight.

We arrived safely at the square of which the nursery formed the rear. How small and insignificant it now appeared to me! Mr. Rogers received us at the door; the nurses, Miss Bella among them, welcomed us most heartily, the little ones crowded around us, but although I enjoyed this greeting, I felt disappointed in a measure. I had expected to be thrilled by a more intense sensation of pleasure, and the reality was less than the anticipation. I had already outgrown the nursery, and even the charm of old friendship vanishes in course of time. I felt too old to play with these little tots; I had a new sensation of diffidence and with the overwhelming self-consciousness of childhood I felt that to play with these other children would have lowered me in their eyes as well as my own. I, usually, preferred the company of younger ones to that of older ones, but these little ones were yet dressed in kilts and I wore a uniform. That made quite a difference. They were babies, while I was a school boy. We stayed just long enough to enjoy the admiration of our former teachers; and we departed earlier than I expected to leave the place with the promise to call again. This promise was given in good faith but after a time, our visits to the nursery grew less frequent until they ceased altogether.

Mr. Rogers led us now to the adjacent wing in which my mother, her husband, and Dr. Leete, my grandfather — (Mrs. Leete had died a few years ago) — had their private apartments. The square in which they lived, was inhabited mostly by members of the medical profession, including hospital nurses. After serving a few hours a day in the hospital, they would return to their homes and use their leisure time as they pleased. Some of them, like my grandfather, who had retired from active service, would spend their time partly in study, partly in travelling.

From Mr. Rogers, I learned the reason why neither my mother nor Dr. Leete had ever come to see me in school. My mother had been sick and my grandfather had just returned from a trip. When I entered the room, I found that mother was quite pale; she held a little baby-girl in her arms. She told me that she was my new sister and that her name was Edith. We found my grandfather in an adjoining room, stretched upon a sofa, reading. Both my mother and grandfather seemed surprised that I looked so well. The latter asked me a number of questions which I answered to the best of my knowledge, although I did not understand their drift. He also placed an instrument at my bare chest and back, and listened through it at my respiration. Then, with a knowing look at my mother, he said; "Julian will live to be an old man, unless he meets with some unforeseen accident."

Mr. Parkman, the gentleman who used to accompany my mother when she came to the nursery, was not at home that day, he was on duty.

I expressed the desire to see the house and my grandfather volunteered to act as our guide. The house did not vary much in its structure and appointments from the rest of the houses, not even from the school. The underground floor contained a natatorium and the usual sanitary accommodations; the floor above it was divided into three parts: Kitchen, dining-hall and library, all of which were sumptuously furnished. One half of the second floor formed the parlor, and the other half as well as the entire third floor, to which the tenants ascended by means of elevator cars, was divided into suites of two and three rooms, which served as bed-chambers for the residents.

Passing through the rooms and corridors, we met a number of people who all expressed their pleasure at seeing "Young West" in such good health. I observed that some of them wore ribbons of various colors in their buttonholes, and my grandfather explained that these ribbons were tokens of public recognition for some extraordinary service which the wearers had rendered to the community. He himself, wore the blue ribbon, which high honor had come to him through the discovery of a specific that would cure cancer, a disease which, heretofore, had been considered incurable. He hoped that some day I would become the recipient of the thanks of the community and be decorated with at least a white ribbon.

This suggestion remained forever in my mind. It recurred to me when after many efforts and many failures in these later years I finally succeeded and the blue ribbon was publicly tied to my buttonhole.

We returned to my mother's apartments and after she had promised to return my call at an early day, we took our leave to see the relatives of my friends. The incidents of these visits were of a similar nature.

At lunch time, we entered the nearest dining-hall. Milton produced his passports and we received about the same fare that we did at school. We observed, however, that the grown up folks would order a variety of dishes which we had never seen before or tasted. Our little mentor informed us that it was not well for children to partake of all kinds of food but that our promotion to high school at the age of fourteen would include also the privilege of ordering for dinner whatever we pleased.

We spent an hour or so walking through the streets and parks until we felt tired, and then we took a public carriage that brought us to the hippodrome.

In my time, the building was not nearly so large and magnificent as it is now, but even then it seated more than fifteen thousand persons, around the immense arena. Three performances were given each day, one in the morning, one in the afternoon, and one during the evening. There were walking matches, bicycle races. and horse races. Trained animals showed their tricks; men and women performed feats of agility, endurance, and strength, and the exhibition closed with the production of a comic pantomime which was greatly enjoyed by us children, who had never seen anything like it before. Milton had visited the place several times and gave us the benefit of his knowledge. He was quite a critic in our eyes and we allowed ourselves to be led by his riper judgment.

He declared the show was "immense," and that
satisfied us.

The hippodrome had been lit up with thousands of electric lights during the performance,
thus we did not observe that night was approaching. When we left the building, we
found it was night, but the city was ablaze
with lights and what a magnificent sight that
was! The walls of the houses, made of stained
glass, showed the most beautiful pictures, mostly
historical scenes, some of which Milton was able
to explain to us. I saw them afterwards so
frequently that they lost their significance to
me, but I remember how vigorously a few of
them impressed me at the time. One of them
represented the landing of the Puritans at
Plymouth Rock; another was a scene in which
fire and smoke issued out of iron tubes, placed
on two hills. Milton said these tubes were
called cannons or guns. Two sets of uniformed
people, one clad in blue, the other in gray,
struck at each other with long curved knives,
sabres, explained Milton; some of these people
were lying sick on the ground, bleeding from
wounds as I did when Bobby hit my head with
the stone, but nobody seemed to care for them,
quite to the contrary, people role their horses
over them. Milton said this picture was called

the Battle of Gettysburg; that many people had objected to exposing such a barbarous scene to the view of the young, but others thought it was well that the children should form some idea of the folly and the savagery of the mediæval ages, so as not to wish for a return of those times. They would thus learn to appreciate more the higher virtues and nobility of our present glorious conditions of universal peace.

Another picture represented a section of ancient Boston,— the North End. I wondered how people could have ever lived in such hovels, and why the children in the streets looked unclean, hungry and careworn.

If I admired Milton Green, it was that evening. I never suspected him of being so learned and well-informed. He told us that he had read how in ancient times, a few people were allowed to enjoy all the wealth of the nation while the greater number were deprived even of the necessities of life; that the former were called rich, the latter, poor.

By that time we had reached the station, and a few minutes later, we were comfortably seated at our table in the dining-hall of our school. Almost all the excursionists had returned. We were tired and, therefore, we sought our beds earlier than usual.

I passed again a restless night. The day had left too many impressions upon my mind. I dreamt that I was falling from a trapeze, right into the midst of a battlefield; horses were about to run over my body, when Mr. Rogers came to my rescue; he picked me up, but he carried me to the North End where people took away my pretty clothes and dressed me in filthy rags and deposited me at the door of a rickety house.

For the next few days, I looked pale, and Mrs. Howe, to whom I told my adventures and dreams, found it not an easy task to quiet me.

However, the shadows passed by. I went to the city time and time again and I saw all the sights, without ever experiencing similar discomforts.

CHAPTER VI.

Four happy years went by. I had been transferred from one class to another. I had worn with great pride a silver cord around the collar of my jacket and had taken charge of smaller children as their mentor.

We were not promoted as was the custom of the 19th century, in full classes and from one

school to another; on the contrary we under-
went a process of careful sifting. Such of us as
showed similar inclinations and talents were
grouped together in separate school buildings
for instruction and further development. I had
reached my 10th year and had shown a decided
liking for manual occupations rather than for
mental work. I was, therefore, sent with a
number of other boys and girls, who had displayed similar traits, to an intermediate school
in which the general development of faculties
like ours was to receive special attention.

The new school was situated at a greater distance from Atlantis than was the primary
department. If the schools were to adjust themselves to the talents of the children; if the mistake of previous ages was to be avoided, by
which the expanding originalities of a child
were pressed into the unyeilding mold of a uniform course of study; if the various lines of
aptitude were to be respected, it became clear as
daylight that the schools must vary in their characters. The simplest, most economic, and at the
same time, the most adequate arrangement was
found in the establishment of provincial schools
for an intermediary course of study. The nursery was strictly a local concern; the primary
school was a city institution; the intermedi-

aries were spread over a whole province and the high schools were scattered all over the land. The primaries were recruited from the nurseries, the intermediaries drew from the primaries, with the slight difference that the primaries received their pupils from specified districts, while the intermediaries were filled, not according to geographical lines but in accord with the particular talents of the children. The ones, who, like my first mentor, Milton Green, showed tastes for literary pursuits, were sent to an intermediary school where these talents were predominately developed, while my friend Bob, who seemed to care only for work that brought into play his muscular strength, had been assigned to one in which such gifts were turned into proper channels of usefulness; the preponderance of logic that expressed itself in love for mathemathical studies was taken care of in another school, and so were schools established in which aptitudes like mine were carefully and exceptionally treated.

Such rational divisions and subdivisions had become possible since the nation had undertaken the education of its future citizens. Only on such a large scale could useful distinctions be made. These intermediaries, though recruited from all parts of a province with regard to

talents of the children, were not, what in mediæval times, would have been called trade
schools. They did not ignore the necessity of
developing also faculties of a secondary or
tertiary predominance. The one who inclined
toward brain work, was not excused entirely
from muscular work, neither was the one who
preferred the latter, permitted to neglect the
culture of his mind. The schools of this order
differed only in so far from one another, that
better opportunities were given for the broaden-
ing of these particular talents.

The best educators are not infallible and thus
it was expected that once in a while children
would be misjudged. Teachers would sometimes be misled by appearances and assume that
a pupil showed a certain talent, where in fact
there was but a semblance of it; moreover, as
children grow older, their predilections sometimes change. Faculties will suddenly show
themselves at the age of twelve that had never
been noticed before. The intermediary schools
corrected such mistakes and pupils could be
transferred with ease from one of them to the
other. This elastic system resulted in finally
placing every child into his or her proper sphere,
so that, when they entered the high school, at the
age of fourteen, no further changes became

necessary and the school authorities could feel reasonably assured that the individuality of every child had been respected.

The greater distance of the school to which I had been promoted from the city, made trips to Atlantis more expensive. Permits for such visits were, therefore, given only four times a year or on exceptional occasions. None of us, however, seemed to care. Instead, we made frequent excursions to other cities under the supervision of our teachers, and new friends consoled us in a very short time for the loss of former acquaintances.

Only a small number of boys and girls had been promoted with me at the same time to the new school. I did not find many whom I had known in our primary school. Of my nursery friends, I recognized only two or three.

This process of constant sifting and replacing, of scattering us all about, did not of course, permit the formation of lasting alliances. But, what of it? Our interests did not clash with one another's and why should we not feel affection for classmates even after one day's aquaintance? As our experiences were identically the same, it took us but a very short time to come to a full understanding with a new companion.

This constant meeting with different persons had even its advantages; the feeling of shyness and distrust vanished, which in previous ages had made the expression and the extension of good will toward a stranger, impossible.

On my first visit to the city and to the primary school which I had just left, I experienced the selfsame feeling of disappointment that had crept over me when I paid my first visit to the nursery. Within a few weeks, I had outgrown these circles and Mr. Groce, the chief gardener, impressed me no longer with the same admiration with which I used to look up to him. My visits ceased, therefore, after a while.

Our school building was modelled after the plan of our primary school but it was larger in its dimensions. Instead of three stories, each wing was seven stories high, to meet requirements. Both the system and the discipline were similar to that of the primary department. The boys of the senior class acted as officers, each supervising five pupils of the three lower classes. This left a number of them unemployed and out of these were chosen commissioned officers, each in charge of five squads. At the head of each company, stood a special officer and another at the head of each battalion, which numbered when in full strength, 125, including himself. Each officer reported to his superior and the chief of a battalion, to one of the teachers. The same arrangement held good also for the girls who took their meals and lessons jointly with the boys.

They learned to handle hammer and chisel as well as the boys, while we learned how to thread and use a needle or how to set a table as well as the girls. Only their dormitories were situated in a different wing of the building and stood under the sole control of women. The girls also had a natatorium of their own, which, however, did not prevent them from taking occasionally a swim with the boys in a lake near the school.

The mode of instruction was also similar to that of the primary school. Lessons were imparted directly through the teacher and not by means of text books. Teacher and class worked together; the teacher showing how to master a certain fact by observation. In the study of geography our memory was not crammed with a thousand names of cities, mountains, rivers or lakes that existed somewhere in the interior of Africa, but, instead, we learned, how to find our way to any given place in the neighborhood by using maps. Every

one of us was able to draw a map of his surroundings at sight, which containing a clear
description of the situation, could be read with
ease by the rest of us. When an excursion on
foot or on bicycles was planned, the map of the
territory to be visited was studied beforehand;
each of the excursionists made a general sketch
of it for his own use and though we left the
school in various groups of not more than
thirty, there was no fear that we would ever
fail to meet at a given point. On our way, we
verified our maps, and when dismissed, we
found our way home without the aid of our
teachers. These excursions extended sometimes over a circle of one hundred miles in
diameter and lasted from five to ten days.

Neither was our memory overloaded with
names of animals, stones, and plants, or with
anecdotes, more or less true, describing their
characteristics. We simply learned how to
observe every object and how to note its qualities. A flower was placed in the hands of a
pupil and he would at once notice its similarity
with or difference from other plants and describe them in every detail.

We never returned from our excursions empty-
handed; we always brought some object that
excited our curiosity, and about which we de-

sired further information. If a clear distinction between our system of teaching and that of previous ages is to be given in a few words, it could be formulated into the following sentence: Heretofore, the teacher questioned the pupil, now the pupil questioned the teacher. All reasonable questions were answered. Either the explanation was given in a straightforward manner or ways and means were outlined by which the pupil could go to work to find out for himself. Foolish questions received no reply, and as this was a rebuke, they rarely occurred.

We had learned how to read and write, but while we were utilizing these acquisitions, we were now taught also a system of writing by which we could note down sentences as rapidly as they were spoken. We also practiced writing by machine. This latter knowledge proved to be of great usefulness because all our telegraphs were manipulated by similar keyboards and all official communications were sent by telegraph.

The English language had so far been the only language which we had studied. We learned how to use it properly and artistically but in the intermediary school, we were now taught a new language — Volapük — by means of which we became enabled to interchange thoughts with the various nations on earth.

Living languages are constantly changing and even the same language is used differently by people of various provices ; it was, therefore, thought best that every nation should preserve its own idiom, although the rapidity of locomotion had made them almost next door neighbors. It would have been a waste of time, and an unbearable tax on the memory, if a person should have been obliged to study half a dozen or more languages. Pupils studied, therefore, simultaneously with their own native dialect, the international language — Volapük. Within one year, we attained such proficiency in it, that no matter at what point of the globe we might have been dropped, we would have been able to converse with the inhabitants.

Our hands had learned to use the simpler tools while in the primary school, now we were made acquainted with the principles of machinery and learned how to apply them to all purposes. We were shown how to divide labor, and how by placing a load upon the shoulders of the many, it could be carried with ease.

No work was undertaken merely on account of its value as a means of instruction. All that we did, was done for a purpose, for results, that

would benefit the community. The several
hundred acres of land attached to every school,
were cultivated by its inmates; the machine
shops turned out articles that were in fact used
by the pupils. Only in so far did they differ
from the ordinary national factories that the
pupils changed off in their various occupations,
while the workers in the latter remained steadily
at one branch of work.

Even our meals were prepared under proper
supervision by a delegation of boys and girls
who changed twice a week. Other squads had
to serve at table, all taking their turn.

While every one of our studies was a labor
and every labor served as a study, we were
allowed an abundance of time for recreation.
We learned how to save minutes and thus we
gained hours of leisure, which we could apply to
sports of all kinds. Time never dragged; we
never felt bored; neither did we ever suffer
from mental or physical exhaustion.

We enjoyed the best of health. Our hospital
attended to but few temporary inmates; the
serious cases were despatched to the city hospitals, and accidents were of rare occurrence.
Our machines were constructed with such care
and foresight that usually it was only through

culpable negligence that a person could possibly get hurt.

The superintendent of each school was held responsible for the general health of his school. If his report showed a larger number of cases of sickness than was normal, an investigation was at once ordered, and if it was found that by better care on his part, they could have been prevented, he was at once discharged from his office and assigned to another position where his responsibilities did not demand capacity of so high an order.

Our schools were the cynosure of all citizens ; they were jealously watched over by all because the future welfare of the commonwealth depended upon them.

At the time when my father was a schoolboy, I learn from his memoirs — each pair of parents interested themselves only in the welfare of their own children ; as long as they were well taken care of, they took little concern in the well-being of the rest, or if they did, in so far only as it stood in relation to their own children and was likely to influence them.

I offered an excellent illustration of the fact that parents can never be trusted to discern the true faculties and the talents of their children, and that only the eye of a talented and at the same time, unprejudiced educator is able to judge the innermost nature of a child and to direct his yearnings into proper channels.

My mother, as well as my grandfather, seemed to be, if not disappointed (for that they were too reasonable) at least surprised at my preferences. Dr. Leete had expected that I would either take to literary pursuits or develop executive ability for practical business; my mother had been sure that I would show abilities to fit me for a nurse or a physician. If I had been brought up under their special care, as was my father by his parents, they would, undoubtedly, have exercised an influence over me with their hopes and wishes in such a manner that I, myself, would have believed myself fit for the occupations which they suggested to me.

Mr. Rogers had already observed that my talents were of an entirely different nature. What they would be, he could not yet tell with exactness, but that I showed a liking for manual pursuits, he felt sure.

Mr. Peters confirmed his observations; the older I grew, the more I showed that muscular exertions were more to my taste than mental occupations. If the mind was to be called into service, some work of the hands had to be added to it, in order to afford me pleasure. Chemistry, for instance, fascinated me because it gave employment to both my mind and my hands. Still I cared less for its theories than for its application to agricultural pursuits.

Mr. Gordon, the principal of the intermediary school, in which I now lived, guided somewhat by my records from the nursery and the primary school, noticed how, as I advanced in years, these two qualities began to blend. He neither stimulated this process nor did he impede it; he gave it free play, allowing me the employment I liked best and excusing me as far as was permissible from studies which did not correspond with my tastes.

Our teachers were lovable and I can hardly decide now whom of them I loved most. They were,— as were all the teachers,— experts in their special branch of instruction. It was, therefore, quite natural that they should put their whole soul into their work and thus weave a spell around us while we were under their influence. Of course, we felt greater attachment to the ones under whom we studied than to those who taught parallel classes, but as we frequently came in contact with them, especially in excursions, we were attracted to them in proportion to our congeniality of tastes and disposition.

The relations that existed between classmates were cordial. Some, it is true, were more sympathetic to one another and antipathies were not overcome entirely, but while the formation of clubs was encouraged of such as were sympathetic, antipathies were not allowed to assume or to degenerate into hostility. The few, for whom one cared less, were simply left to themselves, and they in their turn formed alliances which were congenial to them. There was room for all kinds of selections. Among the thousand inmates, we could easily find a number of friends. Any instinctive dislikes or discords of temperament were weakened partly by the fact that the characters that did not appeal to our fancy were lost in the crowd, partly by way of links. While I might harbor a feeling of antipathy, — for which I could give no reason — towards a certain boy or girl, a sympathetic friend of mine might happen to be attracted by the very same person that I was uninterested in, or disliked. Such a mutual friend would bring us nearer to each other so that our aversions were, at least, kept within proper bounds.

Rivalry existed. Why should it not ? It is

the spice of life. We endeavored to excel one
another in doing our best. It was an honor to
win in a race, or in a game, or to turn out the
most perfect work, but our rivalry was built
upon the appreciation of merit. Besides the
feeling of satisfaction, of having done his best,
or having won the admiration of his classmates,
to which was joined the appreciation of the
teachers, the victor expected no personal advantages from his victories. The defeated party
would always be the first to acknowledge defeat
and to congratulate the winner, while the winner would acknowledge in turn, the merits of
his vanquished opponent. Thus the sting of
defeat was robbed of any bitterness or poison.
Neither were the strong ever pitted against the
weak; and to show exultation because they
were stronger or more clever by nature than
others, would have been bad form. If nature
had given to any one a superiority over others
in a certain branch, such superiority was to be
applied to help the weaker brother. If I could
swim better than another, it was my duty as
well as my privilege to watch over him, while
we were bathing, so that no mishap should
occur to him. If he could stand the strain of
handling his shovel for a longer time than I, it
became his duty as well as his privilege to help

me finish my task. Nature does not create men equal, but man can lift himself by his intellect above nature, mend her shortcomings and divide the common burden so that it will not rest with its whole weight upon the shoulders that are the least capable of carrying it.

Occasionally, delegations from our school would visit other intermediary and primary schools, while we would receive guests from schools equal to ours in rank and from high schools; such visiting and reception days were red letter days, both for the visiting party and the school that was visited. Our guests would give us an exhibition of their skill in the large hall, and we would show them our school and its environments.

Inasmuch as each of our schools represented by their very nature a different course of instruction, and in their pupils a different class of faculties, we could not measure our attainments by a common standard. Our guests, therefore, seemed to know many things of which we were ignorant, and again they were often found lacking in branches of knowledge in which we showed proficiency. As they appeared to us, so we appeared to them, but this very difference destroyed in us every feeling of hostility into which rivalry between schools so easily degenerated in my father's time. We admired the talents of our visitors without deprecating our own.

Visitors from a neighboring school delighted us one evening with a dramatic performance; at another occasion, our guests would surprise us with the lightning rapidity with which they solved arithmetical problems. We, in return, were admired by them when we remodelled their garden-beds or handled a new machine. On one of our visits to a neighboring school, our squad built for them a fountain, bringing the water in drainpipes from quite a distance. To accomplish the task, we stayed with them for a whole week and the admiration of our spectators amply repaid us for our exertions.

When at the beginning of the fourth year, I was promoted into the senior class, I was unanimously chosen by my young friends to command a battalion. The teachers ratified the election and a strip of gold braid was sewn around the collar and the sleeves of my gray uniform. I had earned this distinction partly because I was always found ready to compromise, partly because I was quick in action. When the result of the election was announced, three cheers were given for "Young West," which was another token of love which my classmates had for me.

The honor was, of course, coupled with responsibilities: I had to hold all the subaltern officers under my charge to their, duties, which meant that I had to aid them whenever.I found they were not able to do their part of the work satisfactorily.

About that time, something happened which opened a world of new thoughts to me. To be understood, I must give a detailed account of the occurrence.

CHAPTER VII.

One morning, after breakfast, when, as chief of my battalion, I reported to one of the teachers the occurrences of yesterday, I received orders to present myself at the office.

Mr. Gordon handed to me a despatch from my mother which bade me come to the city without delay. Grandfather Leete had been removed by death. He had suddenly expired without pain or sickness; the cord of his life having been quietly snapped at the end of seventy-five years. The cremation of his body was to take place the following day.

I received leave of absence for three days

with papers that covered my comfortable support during the time.

On my bicycle, I reached the next tunnel station, changed cars at * * * and an hour later, I arrived at Atlantis. I hastened to my mother's residence.

At my mother's I met her husband and my sister Edith, a girl of eight, who had been called from school as I had been. Another son of my mother, Edward by name, was at the time in the nursery. I knew all these relatives of mine because I had met them as often as I visited the city in return to calls which mother as well as grandfather was in the habit of paying me from time to time at school. During his last visit, the latter seemed to have felt the approach of death; he brought me a token by which to remember him, a portfolio, containing lectures composed by my father. They had been intrusted to him with instructions to place them into my hands when I would be old enough to understand their rare character. Fearing that he would pass away suddenly, and that the book might fall into the hands of others, he wished to make sure and gave it to me sooner than he had intended.

Owing to the circumstance that my mother had chosen an occupation that was related to his life's work, they had always lived near each other and thus a feeling of sincere friendship had sprung up between them. Dr. Leete was also the father of two sons, but they had been called away through their choice of occupation to distant parts of the country, and although they paid him their respects by occasional visits, their relations to him or to my mother, their sister, were less intimate.

When the news of their father's death reached them, they came at once by aeroplane to attend the cremation ceremonies. I saw them for the first time, but they had heard of me and were anxious to meet " Young West." The whole family congratulated me upon my election as head of a battalion, and expressed the hope that the gold braid which I now so proudly wore, would not remain the only mark of distinction which I would deserve and receive.

One of my uncles was an expert mathematician. He was employed in the capital as accountant. The other was an electrician and superintended one of the large ocean turbines in Rio Janeiro. Turned by the ebb and tide of the ocean, his turbine produced all the electricity that was needed in that district. They questioned me about my school affairs and found that since their days, many improvements had been inaugurated. They described to me scenes of their school life. None of them had ever been a commissioned officer; they had worn the silver cord but never the gold braid.

My uncles had been in Atlantis about fifteen years ago, at the occasion of my father's funeral. They stated frankly that they had then come only to gratify their curiosity. My father had been a stranger to them, but they had read so much about him that they desired to verify the accounts by direct inquiries. I listened with great interest to all they said, especially when they explained to me the kind of work in which they were employed.

The hour for the ceremonies was set at 10 o'clock the next morning, and at the appointed time, we took a conveyance to the central crematory, where the obsequies were to take place. It was situated on Beacon Hill, on the same spot upon which at my father's time, the government building, called the State House, stood; the two others were placed at the extreme ends of the city. I had frequently passed them but I had never been inside of either of them.

The central crematory was considered one of the finest in the land. It was not built like the rest of the buildings of glass, its walls were

made of what we call stone-pudding, a mixture
of cement and sand. While in a soft condition,
this material can be pressed into wooden molds.
After a few days it hardens and its durability
increases with age.

A flight of stairs, ornamented with appropriate statuary, led to a gallery, supporting a
glass roof upon daintily molded columns. From
this gallery, a number of doors led into the
interior, a large hall, which received its light
partly from above through a huge cupola of
glass, partly from clusters of electrical lamps.
Seats, rising in amphitheatrical form, surrounded a platform of lacquered aluminum upon
which stood on a trap door, a casket made of
asbestos. A neat chancel arose in the rear, to
which the speakers ascended upon winding
stairs.

The casket contained at this hour the body
of Dr. Leete. A wreath of laurel rested upon
the half opened lid. Crossing the platform to
the seats which were reserved for relatives and
the most intimate friends, we cast a last glance
upon his well known features. His eyes were
closed as in sleep.

He had worn the blue ribbon, therefore, the
heads of every governmental department, domiciled in Atlantis, had been convened. They

filled a whole section of the hall. The medical guild had turned out in full force and occupied another section; the guild of hospital nurses was represented by a large delegation; literary clubs of which the departed had been a member, had sent their representatives; people, who had been cured by his medical skill, showed their gatitude by their attendance.

Two hours are granted to each funeral party and as it takes almost fifteen minutes to reduce the body to ashes, and fifteen minutes are usually spent in preliminary arrangements, such as the seating of guests, etc., the exercises cannot be extended beyond the limit of one hour and a half.

An orchestra, hidden from sight, now began to play a dirge, after which, a member of the government, also a wearer of the blue ribbon, ascended the pulpit.

In eloquent words, he extolled the merits of the departed and expressed the gratitude which the world owed him for the valuable services rendered.

Other speakers succeeded him; one described Dr. Leete's career both as a citizen and physician, another spoke of his lovable character and how he had cured people and removed suffering, almost as often by his cheerful presence at the bedside of a patient as by specifics.

The last orator, speaking of the future, referred to the various beliefs that people harbored in regard to personal continuity.

"Death," said he, " is as much a mystery to us in our day as it has always been to mankind. If matter is indeed indestructible, how can the forces which permeate it, cease to be? In fact, matter cannot exist without mind, nor mind without matter, they are one, but whether the same atoms which compose a certain body, or the same forces which dwell therein as mind, will continue in their combinations; whether their number will increase or decrease, or in other words, whether we will remain personalities, no matter in what form, we do not know and never will. To deny a personal existence after death, is as presumptuous on our part as to affirm it."

"If there are some who lead a noble life, inspired by the belief that it is preparatory to a new state of existence, why should we rob them of their happiness by demanding a proof for their assertion, which they can never give? If there are others who feel satisfaction in the thought that death is the end of individual, or personal activity; that the atoms will disband in order to form new creations, or that the forces that inhabit them as mind, will now enter into other forms to do similar service, why shall we demand of them to accept theories of personal continuity for which they find no room in their reason?"

"Neither the past nor the future must concern us, it is the present for which we must have a care. If a personal state of existence does await us after death, so much more pleasant will be our disappointment. We will then accommodate ourselves to the new conditions, as we were forced to place ourselves into proper relationship with the conditions here on earth."

"To live nobly and to enjoy fully the one life of which we know most, must be our foremost aspiration, and by our work to aid contemporaries and co-workers that they may enjoy the measure of time assigned to them, as we do, must be our foremost duty."

"However, as the past has prepared for our welfare, so must we prepare for the well-being of the generations that are to come after us. As we have profited by the labors of our progenitors, so let our children profit by ours."

"Our departed friend has fully understood his duties and he has worked in accordance with such understanding. His studies were ever devoted to researches how to remove pain and how to prolong life to its utmost limits.

He has conquered a disease which had baffled
the skill of the most learned medical men.
The results of his studies will live, therefore, to
the end of time. Thousands of sufferers will
praise him, and thank him for the years of life,
which through his discovery, have been added
to theirs. His name will be mentioned with
reverence and gratitude by our remote descend-
ants, when ours will be long forgotten. Such is
immortality indeed!"

By some invisible mechanism, the casket
slowly sank from sight. The trap door
through which it had disappeared, closed noise-
lessly. The music died away in a plaintive
Adagio, executed by a few string instruments.

About fifteen minutes passed when the folding
doors opened and an urn, containing the ashes
of Dr. Leete, appeared upon the platform.*

The leaves of the laurel wreath that had
decorated the casket were now distributed
among the nearest relatives of the departed. I
received one and afterwards placed it in the
portfolio which Dr. Leete had given to me.

That night, I was unable to sleep. Whether
the imposing ceremonies of the cremation had
excited me; or whether every piece of furniture

---

*All urns are deposited in the city mausoleum, one of the fin-
est structures in the land.

in the room brought back to my memory the kindness which my grandfather had always shown me, I cannot tell. My thoughts wandered from one subject to another.

What was death? I had frequently observed the cessation of life in plants and animals; I had seen flowers fade and wither; I had found birds lifeless in their cages; I had seen chickens, lambs, calves, and once a cow slaughtered to be prepared for the table of our teachers, but I had never before seen the corpse of a human being. What did the orators refer to, when they spoke of a future life, of immortality, of the indestructibility of matter and mind? I began to remember a number of occurrences to which before I had never given a thought.

Once, one of my schoolmates was transferred from the school to the city hospital. He had always been a feeble boy and was troubled with a painful cough; we used to lead him to the sunniest places in the garden and to help him in all his tasks, which he wished to perform, although the teachers had gladly excused him. He went and never returned to school. We were told that he died. Was it painful to die?

While we were swimming in the lake, one day, a little girl suddenly uttered a scream and sank below the surface of the water. By instinct, I dived, caught her, and drew her to the shore. There she lay inanimate. The teacher in charge carried her to the hospital, praised me for my prompt action and said that if I had not been so quick, she might have died ; now he hoped to revive her. The doctors rubbed her with warm towels, and after a while she opened her eyes. For a day or two, she stayed in the hospital, but after that she was as well as formerly.

I asked her how she felt when she sank and why she clung so heavily to me, when I tried to help her, so that I was almost dragged down by her weight. She remembered only that her limbs had suddenly grown stiff while swimming ; more she could not tell ; she had experienced no pain, and was rather astonished when she found herself in bed.

Another schoolmate of mine had fallen from a tree ; he had bruised his head and had sustained some internal injury. The blood oozed from the wound, and we heard him scream with pain until the doctor applied some medicine which put him to sleep. He had been sent off during the night to the City and he never came back. He, too, had died.

All these recollections passed through my

mind. Why did one die and not the other? That a wound causes pain, I knew, because I had been hurt several times, but does it hurt a great deal when one dies? And another question troubled me: did grandfather feel that he was burned to ashes? I was sure that all his good friends, who loved and admired him so much, would not have caused him pain, yet, I could not rid myself of the thought.

I was glad when morning dawned; I arose early and walked up and down the park.

Mother asked me after breakfast whether I would care to own some of Dr. Leete's personal property, perhaps a book. I cared not for books and there was no article among his things, the possession of which would have pleased me. She retained a manuscript of recipes which he had collected, her brothers found nothing of special interest to take with them and thus were all his private possessions delivered to the nation. His valuable books were divided among the public libraries; his instruments, among hospitals; useful pieces of furniture were repaired and offered for sale; such as were useless, were destroyed.

After I had seen my uncles depart by aeroplane to their homes, I took leave of my mother and returned to my school.

I hoped to enjoy a good night's rest after the fatigues of my journey, but again I tossed about and strange thoughts crossed my brain.

I began to wonder how all things sprung into existence. I went from the chicken to the egg, and from the egg to the chicken, from the oak to the acorn, and from the acorn to the oak without even finding an end to the chain.

I knew that the sun would set in the evening and rise in the morning, we had been shown how that happened through the revolutions which the earth makes around its axis, but *why* does the earth turn in that manner? What force moves it in prescribed circles? Who orders it to revolve and the sun to stand still all the while? In a word, the old, old questions over which the wise of all nations had vainly pondered, began to disturb the peace of my mind.

Finally towards morning, I fell into a dreamless sleep and for the first time in my life, I did not hear the music of the orchestrion. My neighbor, observing that I was still in bed, and fast asleep, shook me by the arm. "Young West," said he, when I stared at him in surprise, "what ails. you?" I collected my thoughts, jumped out of bed and hastened to attend to my various duties.

I felt that I must do something to regain my
former state of mind and it occurred to me that
it might be wise to draw one of my classmates
into my confidence, even at the risk of being
laughed at by him.

Everett Brown, one of my classmates, was also
at the head of a battalion, and we were of about
the same age. He was perhaps two or three
months older than I, but he was almost a
head taller. Otherwise, we were equal in muscular strength, in agility, and as was the most
natural outcome of our system of sifting, we
had the same likings for manual labors.

That evening, I invited him to take a walk
with me. We went to the top of a neighboring
hill where we seated ourselves under an elm
tree. That place was a favorite spot of ours;
a most beautiful landscape spread before our
eyes and from there we used to watch the sun
setting behind the western hills.

" Evie," I began, " don't laugh at me, if I ask
a few foolish questions. Since I returned from
Atlantis, serious thoughts have been troubling
me. You know that I went to see the cremation
of my grandfather who has just died; now, I
wonder, is it painful to die? Can you tell
me who created all we see. Of course, a great
many things are done by us, but though we may

put a seed into the ground, we cannot make it grow. Who does? Have ever such thoughts upset your mind?"

Everett was a good natured boy, he could climb a tree like a squirrel, he was one of the best bicycle-riders in the class ; he was neat in his appearance, but he was not quick of comprehension. He stared at me as if he feared for my sanity. Then he answered slowly: " No, I never thought of it nor can I see that it is any of my business or yours to worry about such matters."

" But," I exclaimed, "I never invited such thoughts, they came all by themselves and they will not go unless I find some solution?"

Everett shook his head incredulously; he evidently had never experienced such a sensation. However, he seemed to feel for me, and his good common sense suggested the only and best advise which he could give me.

" Why do you ask me," he said, "I am not older than you, why do you not ask one of the teachers? There is Mr. Gordon, the principal, who ought to know, and there is Mr. Brandon, our instructor of natural sciences, who could give you the desired information."

" A happy idea," I said, " but I am afraid my

questions are so foolish that they will not answer them."

"I should not wonder but that the same thoughts have occurred to some of our classmates," said Everett, "if a number of them were to make the inquiry and you would act as spokesman, I feel assured that our teachers would listen to us."

I reflected a while. "Well," said I finally, "ask the boys; let us hold a meeting and decide what would be the best for us to do."

To this he agreed. On our way home, we discussed the plan in detail how to approach our classmates and pacified by the hope that these troublesome questions would be answered by one of our teachers, I slept that night quietly and awoke the next morning, refreshed in mind and body.

CHAPTER VIII.

To Everett's gratification and to my own pleasant surprise, we found that there were quite a number of boys who were passing through the same crisis. They were not only willing, but eager to obtain an answer to these questions, which, in their opinion, were not

foolish at all. Our teachers had frequently
told us that we ought to examine all subjects
with care, in order to know all about them,
and in difficult cases to ask their aid, which
they would willingly give. Some of the boys
thought that in so important a matter, we
should address the principal of the school; a
greater number, however, felt assured that Mr.
Brandon would be ready to answer our questions. This teacher had frequently accompanied us on our excursions and had always been
so companionable that we forgot he was one of
the teachers and would talk to him as we would
to a classmate. It was, therefore, voted to
approach Mr. Brandon. A committee of three
was appointed to see him and to explain to him
the situation. Of course, I was to serve as
spokesman of the committee.

The very next day, after Mr. Brandon had
just finished a lesson and our class was about to
leave the room, to permit the entrance of
another section, we approached and in a few
words, told him of our errand. We had antici-
pated he would think our questions nonsensical,
or advise us to try and solve them for ourselves.
Mr. Brandon, however, smiled very pleasantly,
placed his hand affectionately upon my head
and said: " I shall be delighted to converse

with you upon that subject; where do you
propose to meet, and at what time?"

"Would it please you to meet us this evening after supper under the old elm tree upon
the hill?"

"That's the very spot and the very hour,
which I would have suggested," said he. "You
may count upon my presence."

Quite a troop of us were seen that evening
wending our way to the top of the hill.

Reserving the bench for Mr. Brandon, we
stretched ourselves upon the soft grass, but
he declined to accept the seat of honor and
threw himself upon the turf as if he were one
of us. "Consider me," said he, "a comrade
and do not hesitate to express your opinions."

I stated again to him my experiences, and by
some clever questioning on his part, he found
that the same thoughts had risen of late in the
minds of other boys.

"To state matters clearly," he said, "you
are eager to know how this universe in which
we live has originated and whether death will
end all. Am I mistaken?"

We assured him that this was exactly what
we wished to know.

He placed his hands languidly under his
head, looked up into the sky, which, just then,

was gilded with the rays of the evening sun, and began :

" Do you remember the lessons which I recently gave to you on fishes and how we observed on that occasion in our aquarium their modes of living? One of you, if I remember rightly, exclaimed then: ' Why, they are acting almost as if they knew what they were doing!' and we came to the conclusion that small as might be their compass of intelligence, they possessed a sufficient amount of it to understand their surroundings. Can you remember that lesson and its incidents?"

We could, and some of us began to remind him of the various observations which we had made.

" Very well, " said he, " supposing one of the fishes,— let us imagine the cleverest fellow among them,— should swim so near to the banks that he could watch the birds fly through the air, build their nests and seek their nourishment, do you think that this clever fellow of a fish could understand why these animals prefer the air to the water or why they build nests? Let us suppose, moreover, that this fish had seen ere this, birds of a larger size, that liked the water and could swim thereupon, would even such knowlege make it possible for him to understand the life of birds?"

We thought that it was not likely.

"Would birds," continued Mr. Brandon, "understand the actions of a fish or those of a four-footed animal? or can you tell me why all these animals cannot place themselves in one another's position?"

Various answers were given but they did not quite hit the mark. Mr. Brandon was obliged to supply the answer to his own question.

"They will never understand one another," he explained, "because the mind force possessed by a fish, does not reach further than to supply the requirements of fish-life, while the mind force possessed by a bird or a higher animal, is limited and adapted to its sphere of life. I have endeavored to demonstrate to you the presence of mind in all matter. There is not an atom of matter that is not permeated by mind; the manifestations only of mind will differ. There is mind contained in a grain of sand; it is mind which causes the affinity of chemicals; search all over creation, examine all its forces and you will find everywhere this close combination of mind and matter; a certain amount of the one mixed up with a certain amount of the other."

"If you understand this proposition, you will easily understand the next step which I will

take with you. These combinations, of which
I have been speaking, most naturally include
their limitation. The quantity of mind given
to a mineral, is exactly the amount necessary
for all the purposes of that mineral's existence;
the amount of mind given to any animal or any
class of animals, is the exact amount needed for
the full existence of that species. It reaches to
a certain point, but not farther."

"The mind that inhabits the human being, is
of course finer in quality and larger in quantity
than that assigned to other beings, at least, we
do not know of any being that possesses the
same or a larger amount of it; but nevertheless,
it has also its limits. We cannot expect its
compass to be infinite. You are yet too inex-
perienced and too young to understand me, were
I to describe to you all the manifestations of the
human mind. I can tell you at present only
what the limitations are, beyond which it can
reach as little as the fish can reach the sphere
of a higher class of animal."

"The limitation of a man's mind is, that he
must always move within the circle of cause
and effect. Man cannot think of anything that
is not either the one or the other. One object,
according to his perception, stands in connection
with a whole chain of other objects and the

strongest minds, such as were developed in the great thinkers of the various ages, have not been able either to conceive something appearing within his circle of observation without a previous cause, or to grasp the idea of nothingness. There has never lived a man on earth nor will he ever live who could think of a time when *nothing* existed. It is at this very point where the human mind reaches its limits, beyond it, it cannot go."

" What bearing has all this upon the questions which you desire me to answer? Can you not see that it is the very answer to your inquiry? You wish to know how this marvelous earth, with all its manifold objects, with all the forces that we observe within, came into existence. That question has been asked ever since man inhabited earth, but it never was answered to satisfaction, simply because the limitation of man's mind permits no answer."

" Young West has told us that he has tried to reach the origin of an oak by following the tree to the acorn and the acorn again to the tree that produced it, but no matter for how long a time he would follow the succession of tree and seed and of seed and tree, he could never reach the end. Why not? I will show it to you by another illustration. You have seen a treadmill of wire attached to the cage of a squirrel. The squirrel will creep into the wheel and try to climb upon the wires that compose it. By these attempts, however, the wheel is turned and work as he may, he always remains at the bottom. Precisely in the same manner does the human mind endeavor in vain to overcome its limitations. Strive as we may, we will always remain in the same position."

"It is necessary that you should understand this in order that you may not be misled by conjectures. Innumerable explanations were given in former ages to account for the origin of all things but on closer examination, they all fell to pieces, and mankind remained like the squirrel in the treadmill, in its old position."

"Some said, there was a time when nothing existed, excepting a power, which they called God, and that this power by effort of His will, created the universe. This would be plausible if only the human mind were able to imagine nothingness, or creation by will effort."

"There were others who traced the origin of the universe back to one small cell, which, through some force that was hidden therein, expanded, until this whole universe, with all that it contains, was evolved therefrom. Especially, in regard to this earth, they would tell a

long story, how in the beginning, it was a ball
of fire that had been thrown off from the sun
and which in course of time, passing through
various conditions, had been formed into what it
is at present."

"All such theories are satisfactory for the
moment, but, when you begin to think you
find that the question is not answered at all by
them; it stubbornly stays. We will still ask:
What was the cause of the first cell? Or who
created the very cause that people were accustomed to call God? Add to this the inability
of the mind to think of a time in which there
was absolutely nothing and you will see how
inadequate even the best of these explanations
are to solve the problem."

"With our minds constituted as they are,
hemmed in by the circle of cause and effect,
we will remain forever incapable of grasping
the origin of creation."

We had followed Mr. Brandon, but he must
have observed by our faces that we were disappointed. Indeed, we had expected that he
would know all about the origin of things, that
he could make it plausible to us; now, he not
only declared that he, himself, knew nothing
about it, but that others knew no more, yea, that
this mystery could never be solved to satisfaction.

After a pause, he continued: " Therefore, why, after all, should we trouble our minds in regard to a past that lies so far behind us. It is neither the past nor the future that should give us concern, it is the present. Here is this beautiful world, here is the span of life, granted to us to enjoy, and here is the work by which to make this life pleasant' for ourselves and others. Would the fish not be foolish were he to leave the elements for which he is adapted, to try the life of a bird? Would he not destroy his happiness by constantly yearning to be something else than a fish? Thus it would be useless for us to try to reach beyond the lines that are set as limits' to our mind force. We must accept conditions as we find them and make the best of them. Supposing we were shipwrecked and thrown upon an island in mid-ocean to which never a ship is expected to come, would it not be foolish on our part to brood forever over the past or to live in expectations that never can be realized? Would it not be wiser to explore the island, to see what resources it had, and to make our abode on it as pleasant as possible? Mankind has advanced quite far during the years in which it has inhabited this globe but it has not discovered all. We know but very little of all the

forces that can be utilized to make our abode ot
earth easier and pleasant.   Enough remains for
us to find out, and seeking to increase the stores
of knowledge by the observation of our surroundings is a more promising work and offers
greater satisfaction than dreaming or conjectur-
ing about the possible or probable causes that
brought this earth into existence, especially,
when we consider that the limitation of our
mind does not allow us to conceive any cause as
a "first" cause.   "Think of the present, boys,"
said our teacher, rising to his feet, "and not of
the past."

We all rose and while going down the hill, he
proposed to meet us the next evening at the
same place, provided we wished him to answer
my second question.

I think, I have before stated, that the boys
and girls of our school had been sent there
on account of the preference which they had
shown for practical work rather than for mental
labors. Abstract thinking was not a strong
point with them.   Those who had shown bril-
liancy of mind in the primary school, had been
transferred to institutions where these talents
were to be developed.   In later years, I discovered that the same topic which Mr. Brandon
had discussed with us on the previous night,

was treated more thoroughly to the great delight
of the pupils, and with much better effect in
other intermediary schools, particularly, in the
ones in which literature, history, or oratory,
were the principal features of instruction.

We were a good natured set of boys and girls ;
we delighted in physical sports of all kinds ;
to exercise our muscles or whatever brain forces
we possessed, in some useful work, gave us pleasure. There were few of us who would read
other books than such that contained information in regard to the best methods, how to
execute various kinds of work. Visitors would
find us employed during our leisure hours either
in games, that required physical skill or in some
work from which we derived pleasure. We
would carve models of ships or construct houses
for pet animals, or weave baskets, etc.

My questions had stirred the curiosity of a
few, but clear as were the explanations which
Mr. Brandon had offered to us, they did not
satisfy them, nor was the subject, itself, of
lasting interest to them. To my chagrin, I
found that very few would join me the next
evening when I started to meet our teacher
at the appointed place and my mortification
increased when I missed even my friend Everett
and was told that he had preferred to partici-

pate with a club of boys in a boat race on the lake. I felt really ashamed when so small a body joined our kind instructor and I expressed my regret to him.

Mr. Brandon did not feel slighted by our diminished numbers; quite to the contrary, he seemed gratified to find so many.

"Never mind," said he to me, "you all are young enough and will have plenty of time to return to the same topic. I am satisfied to give you the benefit of my knowledge, but it requires a more matured mind than is yours to dwell upon them for any length of time. The absentees have followed the advice I gave them last night to the letter; they do not worry either about the past or the future, they enjoy the present. However, as long as any one of you will listen to me, or will ask my opinion, you will find me ever ready to satisfy you as best I can."

I expressed my thanks for the trouble he was taking and we seated ourselves around him as on the previous evening.

"I promised," so he began, "to answer, as well as I am able, your second question. If your first one, regarding the origin of all things was a difficult one, your second interrogation is still more intricate. We are sooner ready to

discard the thoughts concerning the past than
such as refer to the future. The question:
" What will become of us after death?" appeals
to us with much greater force than the one:
" What have we been in the past?" By our
very nature, we cling to life and in as much as
nature prevents our escape by the pain which
every violation of normal conditions causes us,
we have come to think that death is accompanied by pains of the highest degree and that
the nearer we approach death the more intense
grows the pain. Your question, Young West:
'Does it hurt to die?' is, therefore, a very
reasonable one. In answer to it, I can say, that
far from being a high degree of pain, death is
the cessation of all pain. As far as pain is concerned, we need not dread or fear the hour of
death. Pain is needed to preserve our lives.
Just imagine for a moment that it would not
hurt you to fall or to cut your fingers, what
would be the consequences? Without knowing
it, you would break all the bones in your body,
cut off your hands, or destroy your eyesight,
thus making existence impossible. It is because
a cut hurts, that you are careful in the use of
tools or because it is painful to fall, that you are
careful not to offend against the stern law of grav-
ity. It may sound queer to you, when I tell you

that the pain caused by a wound is not felt at the place where it is inflicted, but in your brain, to which your nerves, like telegraph wires, carry the news, viz.: that on a certain place, some abnormal conditions are threatening existence. Let me explain that to you by an illustration. If the telegraph wires between two places were cut, no news of an occurrence that happens in the one place could be carried to the other. The telegraph operator in station B. would remain in ignorance of whatever occurs in station A., or, if the operator of station B. is asleep, his instrument can keep on ticking forever without acquainting him with the message sent by the operator of the other station. Precisely the same occurs in the human body. You can have a tooth extracted or an operation performed on your body under the influence of ether and not feel the least pain. Death destroys the receptive forces; no message of distress can, therefore, reach the mind and thus pain cannot be experienced. This, I hope, will answer your question: "Does it hurt to die?"

"But, connected with it, is the more important question; "What will become of us after death?" Here again we reach the limitation of the mind and all conjectures that we may offer, will lack substantiation by fact. I told

you last night, that every particle of matter is
permeated by a certain amount of mind, or
mind force, that in fact, mind and matter cannot be thought of as separate from each other.
There is not an atom of matter without mind
and so can mind not exist except in connection
with matter. In that combination of mind and
matter which we form, the manifestations of the
mind show themselves in the way we are accustomed to find them in a human being, while the
manifestations of the mind force that combine
with matter in the construction of any other
being, for instance, in a tree, or a mineral, or an
animal, show themselves in a different way.
As soon as these peculiar combinations cease or
are destroyed, neither mind nor matter goes out
of existence, they merely enter into new combinations, and these new combinations most naturally, manifest themselves in new forms and
activities. If both mind and matter are indestructible, if they cannot be annihilated, their
places in the universe cannot remain vacant;
they must continue to exist, and only their
manifestations will change from the moment
they become parts of a new combination."

"Perhaps you will grasp the meaning of
the rather difficult lesson I am trying to impart
to you, by means of the following illustration.

You have seen in the laboratory how we dissolve
water into its component parts, hydrogen and
oxygen. In their combination, these elements
form what we know as water, and as water they
become useful to us in a great many ways. I
need not tell you what the properties of water
are, you know them. Not sooner, however,
do we separate the oxygen from the hydrogen,
than the form of water is lost and if we unite
either the hydrogen or the oxygen with some
other chemical, a new substance is created that
shows not even one of the properties that water
formerly showed. We may call the water
"dead" after that separation of its elements,
but does it not exist yet in its parts?. Exactly
in the same manner do we continue after mind
and matter that have composed us and have
manifested themselves for a certain time in our
activities; are separated and enter into new
states of existence."

"Looked upon in that light, we need not dread
the future, whatever that may be, and from
such observations, we arrive at the same lessons
which we obtain from reflections upon the past.
It is the present that concerns us; here we find
ourselves, a combination of mind and matter;
its manifestations we call our life; let us act
that out in the fullest sense of the word and

in accordance with its destination. Let us
recognize its limitation and whatever may become of us after the separation of mind and
matter, we may feel sure that the material of
which we are formed, as well as the forces which
keep them in this prescribed form, will accomodate themselves with the same ease to new conditions as they have to their present."

After he had finished, I looked about and
found that some of my companions could scarcely
keep their eyes open. What our teacher had
told them was more than they could comprehend.

On our way home, Mr. Brandon began to
talk to us about daily occurrences; about an
excursion which we had planned; about the
outcome of a series of baseball-games, that were
played by various clubs; about the recent walking match and other related topics. This conversation had the effect that when we arrived
at home, his lecture on death was forgotten and
did not disturb our slumber.

I was the only one who took the whole matter
in a more serious way. Whenever I found an
opportunity, I had some new question to ask
Mr. Brandon, which he always answered in
a most pleasant manner. He advised me to
read several books, especially the religious text
books of former times, among them, the Vedas,

the Bible, and the Koran. I tried to read them but they were so uninteresting to me that I gave up the attempt.

What surprised me most in them was that they all advised to feed the hungry, clothe the naked, not to take what belonged to others, etc.

Had there ever been people who went without a meal or were lacking clothes? Were there ever people guilty of encumbering themselves with the personal property of others?

One of these books, the Bible, was full of narratives of wars in which one people destroyed the lives and properties of others. The stories ran, that God, by whom, I supposed then was meant a person of great power, helped them in their destructive work. Why did they destroy the ones whose help they needed to produce the good things of this life? I placed this question before Mr. Brandon and he told me that the people of that time had hardly emerged from barbarism and that they acted more like brutes than like human beings.

On the whole, I did not care for that class of literature, I returned the books to the library and not before many years did I touch them again.

CHAPTER IX.

The time finally arrived that I was promoted to the High school. Again the classmates had to part. According to the talents which we had developed, we were sent to continue our studies in such parts of the country as offered the best chances of observing the various branches of production and manufacture for which we had shown a preference. I, with a few of my friends, was sent westward to a school in the neighborhood of Denver, in Colorado. A number of mines from which useful metals are drawn, are found in the near vicinity of that school; there are also large farms, some of them covering thousands of acres of ground.

An aeroplane was ordered for our journey and for the first time in my life, I experienced the sensations which travel in an air-ship offers. The aeroplane rises only to a limited height, not too distant from the earth to hinder obser-vation. 1 need not describe the vehicle to my readers as they must be all familiar with its construction, I merely wish to remind them of the fascinations with which a first journey in one of them, charms the traveller.

We rose higher and higher until the cities below us resembled toys, the people in them, ants in their heaps, the rivers, silver bands, winding through the green, and the lakes pieces of glass scattered over the surface.

The trip lasted twenty-four hours, a night and a day. We started late in the afternoon, and far into the night, we remained on deck enjoying the landscape, illuminated by myriads of electric lights, over which we were passing.

Mr. Brandon had been selected to accompany us and to deliver us safely to the new principal. He had frequently made this journey and was, therefore, familiar with all the objects that met our gaze. He pointed out to us the largest aluminum works and gave us an estimate of the amount of that metal that was used every year and of the number of people who were employed in its manufacture. "In former ages," he explained, "most articles were made of wood, and people were, therefore, always exposed to the dangers of fire. He told us how the city of Chicago, which we passed on our way, was once destroyed by a conflagration and how a good deal of energy was wasted in former days in preparations to subdue this hostile force.

Supper was served and after that we went to rest in the compartments of the ship's dormitory. We were up early because we were eager to see all the novel sights. We crossed a vast plain, upon which, as Mr. Brandon told us, quite a quantity of cerials were raised with which the people were supplied. We observed large tracts of land covered only with grass upon which immense herds of cattle were grazing. All these sights were new to us and our eyes feasted on them.

We also watched with great interest the engineer, who skillfully directed the course of the aeroplane, utilizing the evershifting winds.

We almost met with an accident. A piston in one of our motors broke; the machine ceased to work and we descended so rapidly that we were in danger of striking the ground and wrecking the ship. The helmsman, however, did not lose his presence of mind. He ordered the parachutes to be opened and the rapidity of our downward course was thus broken.

We landed quite a distance from a city, but some people who were working in the fields near by, had observed us and came to our rescue. After a short delay, the machine was repaired and we departed.

As a matter of course, we arrived at our

destination later than we were expected. An investigation took place at once to ascertain whether the accident had been unavoidable or whether it was caused by some culpable negligence. It was proven that nobody was to blame, that the machinery had been examined carefully before we started and that it had been found in good working order.

Mr. Brandon delivered his charge to the principal, a gentleman, who impressed me in the same manner as had all my principals heretofore. Mr. Chase seemed to be kind-hearted and thoroughly adapted for his work. When he looked at us with his large blue eyes, he seemed to penetrate our very souls and read our very thoughts. I was introduced to him by Mr. Brandon as "Young West" and on account of my descent from so famous a father, I was received by Mr. Chase with a somewhat greater attention than that which is usually bestowed upon new comers.

The routine in the school varied little from that of the other schools, and yet there were a few remarkable divergencies.

We were now old enough and sufficiently trained to take care of ourselves; there was no further need of being given in charge of the older pupils of the school. Each class elected

its own officers who were distinguished from the
rest by a silver cord around the sleeves of their
uniform. The commissioned officers were drawn
only from the senior class, and gold braided
shoulder straps were the insignia of their office.
The scholars of the junior class were allowed to
vote for their non-commissioned officers, but they
had no right to cast their ballots for the commissioned officers. It could not be expected
that the new comers should know anything
concerning the qualification of boys to an office,
who were strangers to them. As it happened,
I failed this time to be elected to an office, even
by the contingent that came from our school.
The choice fell upon my friend Everett. I did
not consider that a humiliation, but was rather
glad to escape for a year the onerous duties and
responsibilities that are connected with an
office. Understanding how difficult the task of
an overseer is, all of us, who had held offices
before, yielded understandingly to the authority
of their superiors and tried to make their duties
easier for them.

Another innovation was, that an account was
now opened for us in the books of the school
and that we received expenditure-blanks. Our
clothing and school utensils were furnished for
us as heretofore, but we were now given the

liberty of choosing what we desired to eat from
a bill of fare and to pay for it from the amount
granted to us for that purpose. The sum was
large enough to keep us well fed during the
term of half a year. There were also provisions
made for travelling expenses. Whenever we
planned a trip, each now had to provide for
himself, according to his likings. A margin
was also left for the purchase of articles for
personal comforts or to pay for admission to
hippodromes or other places of amusement,
which we liked to frequent when we visited
Denver. These expenditure slips bore the
stamp of our school and had to be signed by us.
They were issued for the amounts fixed as the
price of the purchased article and we were
warned to arrange our financial affairs in such a
manner as not to overdraw our accounts. At
the end of each term, the amounts were can-
celled and after a short time, we had learned so
well to manage our affairs that none of us were
found short, whereas most of us had a surplus of
funds to return to the treasury.

This liberty of choosing our food, included
also the liberty of asking for meats, which, heretofore, had been denied us. Although I accustomed myself in the course of time to the
use of viands, I cannot say that I became a

great lover of either fish, fowl, or meat. I preferred a vegetable diet and so did a great many
of my companions.

Beverages, containing small quantities of alco-
hol, and light wines, such as are yet liked by
some people and, therefore, manufactured, were
not on our bill of fare, and the keepers of
the national stores were not permitted to deliver
such to the inmates of a school. Not before a
person had entered the industrial army, was
such a privilege extended to him. Later on, as
you know, the privilege was witheld until a
person reached his twenty-fifth year and I can
see no reason why the manufacture of such
beverages should not be discontinued altogether,
precisely as has been the manufacture of nar-
cotics, when the demand for them had ceased.

Another difference between our present school
and the primary and intermediary schools, was,
that girls were no longer educated with us in
the same buildings. There was another school
like ours in the vicinity, entirely arranged for
the education of girls. The two schools in their
work stood in intimate relation to each other,
visits were frequently exchanged and many
of our excursions were undertaken by parties
from both institutions. They, however, occupied their own building as we did ours and their

instructors were now women while ours were men.

This arrangement had been perfected after a great deal of study and so far, we have found it the wisest and the best.

We had not been kept, heretofore, in total ignorance in regard to the process of generation. We had been led to observe it in plants, after that, in animals of a lower grade, finally in animals of a higher order until it was but a short step to take to apply the same laws of generation to the human species. Far from exciting our curiosity or corrupting us, all these observations and the conversations we had about them, had left us rather indifferent, but now that the age of puberty had been reached by us, peculiar sensations and strange feelings began to trouble us. We had seen in the museums and in the large public places in the cities, statues representing the human form in its nudity. So far they had not affected our imagination; now we began to look at them with different emotions. We had strange dreams; in a word, we passed through that stage of life in which nature prepares us for the coming duties of procreation. Our teachers understood this strange process through which we were passing, as they themselves had passed through it, and they instructed us in all the laws by which generation is regulated. After we left the high school, we were fully conver-sant with the mysterious actions of this natural force. All coarseness was removed; the brutal elements had been eliminated and the holiness and sanctity that surrounds that mystery was alone preserved.

Similar instructions were imparted to the girls by their teachers and when we met after-wards as young men and women, we met on an equal footing, thoroughly conversant with the consequences of any rash act, which under the pressure of this most powerful of all natural forces, the young are likely to commit.

We were also told to pay greater attention to newspapers and to periodicals than we had given to that class of literature before. Some changes have occurred in the collection and distribution of news since I was a boy, but in general, our daily and weekly papers were then about the same as they are now.

There was the National News Register, which informed the reader of the events of the day; it announced the official orders; it brought accounts of the decisions of the courts of arbitration; it published the names of people promoted to some higher office; it reported the deaths of all such men or women who had distinguished themselves and were filling or had filled responsible positions.

The Provincial News Register and the City News Register, contained matter of a similar nature with the only difference that their announcements referred to the inhabitants of the city or province in which they were published, but not to the whole country.

Next in order were the publications of the various guilds which appeared weekly or monthly and which discussed pro and con, the latest inventions in their branch of industry. They also contained news matter which was expected to be useful and of interest to the members of such a fraternity.

The schools had a periodical of their own, to which the principals and teachers all over the country contributed. Besides discussions of educational topics, they contained the names of pupils that were chosen to hold offices and it was for honorable mention in such a paper that we gladly took upon us the burdens of an office. Most high schools issued a paper of their own which they exchanged with other high schools so that quite a number of them could always be found upon the tables of our library. These sheets were not alike in volume or composition.

Some of them were quite elaborate while others were rather small and plain. The best, generally, came from the high schools in which literary talents received development and the plain ones from institutions like ours, where literary attainments were not of a high order.

The news was collected by a very simple method. The heads of each department sent their reports either daily or weekly to the press bureau. Here the items were sifted, rubricated and published.

Every member of the guild had the privilege of sending his contribution to the periodical of his order. No matter what his opinion was, or whether it agreed with, or opposed prevailing ideas, it was published in the order in which it was received. An overflow of matter rarely occurred, because nobody cared to appear in public print unless he had, indeed, some novel and good idea to offer. The cost of the manufacture of these papers was small on account of their large circulation, so that the subscription price for such a publication was trifling. A person could order several of them without feeling it. Some agriculturists were interested in news concerning machines and some textile maker desired to follow the progress of architecture. Whosoever wished to be informed only now and then about what was going on in other branches of industry than his own, could find all periodicals in the libraries of either his block or the club to which he belonged.

The paper which we edited and printed in our school was made up entirely by the boys, as in all high schools the labors needed for their proper management were performed by its inmates. We were divided into a number of squads, which under the supervision of either a teacher or an expert official, would take turns in managing the house. While one division would run for a week the machinery of the house, another would attend to the kitchen, a third to the serving of the table, a fourth to the laundry, a fifth to the gardening, etc. The same section, which in its turn was found one week in the laundry, could be found the next week in the printing department or in the offices which connected the school with the supply department or the general government. The labor, divided among so many, became no burden to any of us so that neither were our hours of recreation curtailed by them nor our progress in our various studies impeded.

Besides continuing our former studies, we were now introduced into the science of civil engineering, topography, chemistry and related branches. Numbers of us were also sent in turn to neighboring farms to assist in farm work, or to neighboring mines to become familiar with this branch of labor. Frequent excursions were made to industrial establishments so that there was hardly an article used by us, the manufacture of which we could not explain. Three times during the year, every division was given a vacation of two weeks, which, if they chose, they could spend in travel.

During my stay in the high school, I visited my mother twice, and upon a cordial invitation from one of my uncles, I called once upon him. The trip to South America, which I made in an aeroplane, was rather an expensive one to me and I prepared for it for quite a while, curtailing my expenses in every possible manner. I lived more frugal, denied myself various amusements and remained quietly at home during one vacation, but the new scenes which I saw during that trip and the reception which my uncle gave me, fully repaid me for my sacrifices.

I made many fast friends in the school so that already in my second year, the silver cord adorned my uniform, and in the fourth year I was chosen to one of the highest offices of the school organization. It was at that time when I visited my uncle.

I will not withold the truth from the reader and confess that a feeling of vanity prompted me to show not only my gold-braided shoulder straps but also the white ribbon in my button-hole, which I had received from the government in acknowledgment of a deed of bravery.

I had been detailed, some time before, to work for a couple of days in a neighboring lead mine. By an unforeseen accident, a gallery caved in and a number of men were buried under the debris. A call was made for volunteers to enter the unsafe regions and to try to save them. I offered my services at once. My physical strength and my nimbleness overcame all the dangers that threatened our small party, and I was the first one who reached the unfortunates. It had been one of my qualities to always think before I acted and thus I had the foresight of taking with me some food and water before starting, a consideration which had been overlooked by the rest in the excitement of the hour. I found the men in a terrible condition; some had been killed; a number had been wounded, and the ones who had escaped unhurt, were exhausted from the want of food and, especially, of water. The provisions I brought with me saved their lives. I received therefore, public thanks not alone for my willingness to risk my life in the rescue of others, but for having remained collected and careful, where others, older than myself, had lost their heads. It was then that the white ribbon was given to me and as I was the only boy in our school who had earned a decoration, I felt rather proud of the distinction.

I look back upon the years in high school as the most pleasant in my life. Although I had never suffered from any serious sickness, and although I had developed into a pretty strong boy to the astonishment of all who knew me as a child, my lungs were not as strong as I could have wished them to be. The slightest cold affected me, but since the time that I was transplanted into the bracing climate of Colorado, I experienced no trouble and my respiratory organs improved. I enjoyed perfect health; I grew over night, so that at the age of eighteen, I measured six feet, and weighed one hundred and eighty pounds. The work in which I was employed as well as my studies, gave me great pleasure. Athletic sports also offered me amusement and on account of my agility I was well liked in the various clubs which the boys had formed for their games. I could walk and run without being easily exhausted; I rowed a firm stroke; I was a swift bicycle rider. While working on the farm, I learned to ride on horseback and as I loved horses, it became a favorite pastime with me.

I began now to look forward with joyful anticipation to the time when I should join the Industrial army, because all the boys began to feel when they came to that age that they should do something for the community which so far had cared for them, had so amply provided for their wants, and had permitted them to pass their youth in so pleasant a manner. " Two more years," we said to one another, " to Muster-day," and our faces beamed with delight.

These two years were called the collegiate years, of which one was to be spent in another institution near by, the other in travelling.

CHAPTER X.

Little occurred during these last two years of school life which to relate would interest the reader. The difference between the college and the high school consisted merely that we ceased to wear a uniform and that we had to supply all our wearing apparel from the funds placed to our account. Each could now dress as he pleased, but though our tastes began to differ, as a rule, we dressed in a quiet and simple manner. We would dress more elaborately only when we met girls from neighboring colleges at entertainments; then we tried to look our best. We had been trained in calisthenics already in the intermediary schools, and we continued these pleasant exercises, because the charm and fascination which we experienced in the company of the other sex had grown as we advanced in years.

I had always loved to be in the company of girls and counted many friends among them. Still, I had never met a girl that attracted me otherwise than would a playmate of my own sex. The girls whom I had met so far were all pursuing the same studies as myself; they were similarly talented, and showed the same inclinations for practical work. Our conversations would ever turn around the same topics. They found nothing special to admire in me nor did I in them. They could do the same work that I did and I could accomplish with ease any task assigned to them. As the positive or negative poles of a magnet will repel each other, so do equal talents and aspirations of the same order rarely ever attract the sexes.

I learned to look up to a woman of my age with admiration for the first time in my life when, in my second collegiate year, I was sent travelling to a southern city, in the neighborhood of which I was to study, for a month or two, the culture of the cotton plant.

We met upon a Mississippi boat. Miss Violet Horton was a musician. She was a Californian by birth. In her childhood she had shown a talent for music, which had been developed until finally she was sent to Atlantis, in which city at that time, the highest branches of music were taught. She sang very well, played the harp most excellently, but the instrument which was her forte was the violin. She was travelling to the same southern city in the neighborhood of which I was to pursue my avocation, in order to appear as soloist in a symphony.

I liked music to some extent, but my knowledge of that art was rather limited. I had absolutely no understanding of its higher meaning. A march, played by an orchestrion, with plenty of drums and trumpets in it, or a waltz which would invite the feet to a dance, was more appreciated by me than the finest symphony composed by the most celebrated maestro.

Upon the request of some fellow travellers, she had played for us in the parlor of the boat, and for the first time in my life I felt that there was more in music than I had ever suspected. Her instrument seemed to speak, to laugh and to weep; it expressed joy and sorrow; it appealed to every one of the emotions that dwell in the human heart. She had kept her audience spell-bound during her performance, and a storm of applause greeted her as the last note had died into silence. Tears had even risen to my eyes.

On deck we fell into conversation. My name had been mentioned to her. "You are Young West," she addressed me; "why, I know your mother. During my stay in Atlantis I was taken sick and your mother was my nurse in the hospital."

We spoke of the various sights that were to be seen in the city, of its institutions, of its pleasure resorts on the shores of its beautiful harbor. This led to her telling me of California and to my telling her of Colorado, also of my recent trip to South America. She then turned the conversation upon the great masters of her art, of whom I had but little heard, of the concerts in which she had appeared, and of her prospects and plans for the future. I could

only tell her of my aspirations and of the
occupations which I preferred to all others.
Vanity prompted me to help her discover the
white ribbon which I wore, and I was more
than gratified when she asked me to relate the
adventure through which I had earned that
distinction.

In the same degree as the realms of sound in
which she moved and lived were foreign to me,
so was she a stranger in my spheres of activity;
as I admired her, so she seemed to admire me;
as I overestimated the intricacies of the musical
art, so did she, no doubt, overestimate the difficulties of my pursuits. In a word, her presence
wove a spell around me which I could not break,
and did not care to break.

A peculiar, unpleasant and surely foolish feeling stole over me when several other young men,
fellow passengers on the boat, sought her company and she conversed with them as cheerfully as she did with me. How could I expect
that after so short an acquaintance she should
have neither ears nor eyes for anybody else but
for me alone? I began to sulk and came near
making a fool of myself. With difficulty did I
fight down this feeling of jealousy, in the hope
that, as I was to stay with her in the same
neighborhood for quite a while, our friendship,

from which I derived so much pleasure, might increase.

When we arrived at our destination, we exchanged addresses and she promised to receive me whenever I should choose to call.

A few days passed before I had familiarized myself with the conditions which I had been sent to the place to learn, but though I diligently pursued my studies, I could not tear my thoughts away from the fair musician. I saw her slender form ever before me; the tones which she had drawn from her instrument, were continually ringing in my ears; I remembered with delight the sensation of the touch of her hand on bidding her good-by. I could compare it only to an electric shock.

The plantation upon which I was stationed for the sake of observation was situated at some distance from the city and I had to travel morning and night to and from the place for several hours. Occasionally I had to spend the night with some of the workmen on the plantation. All this made it impossible for me to visit my new friend during the first two weeks after my arrival.

At last, the most difficult of my tasks were accomplished and I could take a holiday. I called on Miss Horton one morning, but was told that she was at a rehearsal. She had taken rooms in a block where most of the musicians domiciled in this city resided. I left my card in the office, naming the time when I would return in the afternoon.

With a few friends, I strolled through the town to see the sights and took lunch at the planters' club-house, but time seemed to hang on my hands. The dials on the street clocks had apparently conspired against me; they informed me that I had plenty of time yet.

When I called at the office I found a note from Miss Horton, regretting that some previous engagement hindered her from receiving me that afternoon, but that she would be pleased to meet me after the concert in which she was to play that evening.

Not being a judge of music, I can tell only that the audience listened with delight to every number of the programme and that my friend's play took the house by storm. In my vanity, I had expected, that when stepping upon the stage, she would at least make an effort to ascertain whether I was in the audience; I tried to catch her eye; she did not seem to care. From the moment she began to play until she had finished, she appeared enwrapped in her art. The ovation that was rendered to her did not affect her in the least; she simply- bow d in acknowledgment like one who is accustomed to receive such expressions of appreciation.

I sent one of the ushers with my card to her, and upon her orders, he led me after the concert to a private room behind the stage, that was reserved for the artists and their friends.   I found her surrounded by men and women of the. musical profession, also by people, who, without being musicians, themselves, were lovers and good critics of music.   They talked about the performance and how the various numbers had been rendered.   All they said was so utterly foreign to me that I almost felt ashamed of myself.

As soon as she caught sight of me, she came pleasantly forward and extended both her hands to greet me.   We exchanged the usual civilities, after which she introduced me to the company. I was thankful to her that she called me " Mr. West," and not " Young West; " still I heard some one whisper: "So! that is Young West, whose father had slept for over a hundred years. His discovery and resurrection created quite a sensation at that time."

Miss Horton asked me to take lunch with her at the Musicians' Club House.   Here we spent more than an hour in pleasant conversation, after which I saw her home. At parting, I invited her to come and see me in my circles, and she cheerfully accepted without hesitation; I was to call upon her the next morning, take her with me to the plantation, and bring her back to the city by the last train.

I went to my lodgings in high spirits. To-morrow, I was to have her all alone to myself, and what was more, I would have a chance to show her what I could do. Such is youth; we think more of the approving smile of the woman who fascinates us, than of the applause of a whole world.

My guest submitted gracefully to my guidance. She listened attentively to the explanations which I offered concerning sights that were novel to her, or agricultural machines which she had never seen. I felt indeed proud to show that I was familiar with all these devices and I used, perhaps abused, every opportunity to exhibit my strength and skill.

After I had finished my task for the day, we strolled through the fields, conversing, as will young folks, on all kinds of topics for which on other occasions, they show not the least interest. The hours sped away; never had evening approached so quickly as on this day. We went to the station, took the train, and when we had arrived in the city and at her residence, she thanked me, saying that she had spent a most delightful day. She suggested another excursion to the same place, in company with some mutual friends. The excursion came off to the satisfaction of all participants. After that, she would visit me on the plantation whenever she had a day to spare, while I never failed to be present at any of the concerts at which she played.

My term came to a close before hers and I received orders to leave and report on a certain day in the city of XXX in which one of the largest chemical laboratories in the country was located, to take a course in practical chemistry.

I had frequently parted from friends, but I never felt the pang which separation from dear ones brings, to such an extent as on this occasion. I notified her of my early departure and she agreed to accompany me to the boat upon which I was to take passage. Awaiting the last signal, we were walking the deck; I felt sorely depressed, and also Miss Horton was not as talkative and cheerful as usual. "It seems to me," said I, "as if I had known you many, many years and yet it is only a short time since we became acquainted."

She nodded assent.

"Will you forget the hours and days which we have spent so pleasantly together? I never will."

"How could I?" said she. "Your company gave me great pleasure, particularly because it revealed to me another side of life. We artists are a peculiar class of people, we revel constantly in dreams and rarely obtain a correct view of the real world in which, after all, we move. Your talk was refreshing to me, because it led me away from the musical world, and if I am grateful to you for one thing, it is that you have abstained from all flattery with which musical enthusiasts disgust us so frequently. Though you never pretended to understand music, or to appreciate it as an art, I always felt when I played to you that it did affect you. I read in your eyes your appreciation of my skill, and that was a greater reward to me than is sometimes the applause of a multitude."

I asked her if she would care to hear from me in the future and whether I might be permitted to hope to hear from her now and then.

She assented cordially to both propositions.

Letters were to be sent by me to Atlantis to the Conservatory of Music in whose charge she still was, and she would write to me to the College which was directing my travels.

The bell rang, we shook hands once more, and she left the boat, waited, however, on the pier, and waived her handkerchief till the vessel had left the slip.

She had entered into my life like an apparition. I wondered a little painfully if she would vanish out of it like a dream?

I had never been fond of writing; two hours' labor in a field or at a work-bench, did not fatigue me as much as a composition or an essay that could be finished in an hour. My friends could never complain that I flooded them with epistles. They rather scolded me for my neglect to answer theirs, and so far, I had never committed the offence of contributing to any of our papers. I was perfectly able to render a clear and brief account of any official mission with which I was intrusted. I could describe an object accurately so that the reader could form a correct picture of it for himself, but otherwise, I lacked literary abilities.

Now my whole nature changed; I took quite a delight in writing long and frequent letters to Miss Horton, describing to her in detail, not alone what I did and said, but even what I thought. I began to be more careful in my expressions and would rewrite letters several times before they suited me. I tried to give them a kind of artistic finish; I would dress the most trivial observations in the prettiest forms I could think of, and when it came to meditations, I simply rose to the sublime; at least I thought so.

I did not know then, as I learned to understand at a later day, that every young man passes once in his life through a stratum of poetry which is of larger or smaller dimensions as individual cases differ, nor did I know at the time that it is Cupid in the disguise of Apollo who inspires us. Poetry at that age, is a sure symptom of the disease commonly known as love-sickness. I was, indeed, in love, though I did not know it.

Miss Horton on her part, informed me of her travels, of her studies, and of her successes. She would mention the names of other renowned musicians, whose fame she envied and whom she tried to emulate. My classmates and co-workers were not unfrequently surprised to find me so well posted in matters of music, for which they never suspected me to possess any taste. Had they known the real source of my information they would have surely made me the target of their witticisms, but I preserved jealously my secret and they traced my knowl-

edge to a musical paper, to which I had of late
taken a fancy to subscribe.

Although Miss Horton was not older than I
was and although I towered far above her in
physical structure, her thoughts were more
matured than mine. In my ideas I was a boy
in comparison to her. On many occasions, I
would ask her advice, which was cheerfully
given and which always struck the nail right on
the head. When I compared her with the girls
whom I had frequent occasion to meet, it
seemed to me that no other woman was as personally fair and attractive as she, although she
was not beautiful, but rather plain looking.

To have her near me as a companion all my
life, I thought would be the consummation of
earthly happiness, as I could rely much better
upon her advice than upon that of anybody else.

All these sentiments had the effect upon me
that I became more sober and earnest in all my
thoughts and deeds. I beheld a goal before me,
after which to reach and strive. I wanted to
do something to distinguish myself, in order
that I might win her confidence, her admiration, her affection. I must not merely do my
duty, I must do something more than was
expected of me. All these reflections, which
charmed me during many a silent hour, did

not, therefore, draw my attention from my work, they rather made me careful in rendering perfect whatever task was assigned to me. I began to yearn more than ever before to enter into practical life and I looked forward with great expectancy toward the day on which my education would be finished and I would begin my life as a member of the Industrial Army.

CHAPTER XI.

Authors write not alone to be understood by their contemporaries, they harbor the secret hope that the products of their pens will give pleasure or instruction to the remotest generations. Thus it is a cheerful dream of mine that my reminiscences will be read not alone by the present generation, but will survive and reach, at least, our great grand-children. It has happened within my own life-time that many changes in our conditions have taken place, so that, what I have heard and seen as a child, is seen and heard no longer by children of the present day. They are merely informed to-day of conditions and usages that have been and are no more. For example, I can remind the readers of my age that in our

days, the annual Muster-day, or to call the thing
by the right name, the annual Muster-week, was
celebrated during the latter part of June, while
now, the celebration of that national festival
takes place in the first week of September; also
that many forms of the ceremonials have been
remodeled. It is therefore, not unreasonable to
suspect that the next century may again change
the features of that day in such a manner that
it will remain barely recognizable to a person of
our age.

I preface this chapter with the above lines to
justify its insertion into my memoirs. I am
aware of the fact that the description of the
scenes and incidents of Muster-week is unnecessary, as all persons above the age of twenty have
passed through it, but there may come a time,
and for that time I am writing, when such a
pen-picture may be a revelation to prospective
readers.

Since the time when it became the duty of
the government to direct the efforts of the whole
nation in their common fight against the real
enemies of mankind, hunger, cold, disease, and
ignorance, the functions of the administration
were divided between a number of departments,
of which each was sub-divided into divisions and
sections. There was the department of food

supply, sub-divided into agriculture, stock-rais-
ing, forestry, fishing. There was the department
of architecture which combined the various
building trades and the construction and preservation of roads, canals and tunnels. There was
the department of manufacture, branching out
in the fabrication of all kind of textiles, into
tanning, shoe-making, and garment working.
We had our department of machinery which
made and operated all the machines necessary to
set the great forces of nature to work. Our
electrical division surpassed anything the world
had ever seen. Another department took care
of the distribution of all products; it supervised
the accounts that were kept with every individual
and superintended the national stores and sam-
ple-houses. We had a department that included
the teachers' profession, and all kinds of instructors, from the nursery maid to the professor of
national economy, from the horticulturist to the
professor of music or painting. The medical
profession, embracing the whole hospital service
of the nation, formed another department and
in a similar manner all the arts were gathered
into one department. I must not forget to
mention the department of transportation as
one of the most prominent. It had charge of
the ships, railroads, and aeroplanes, of tele-

graphs, telephones, and the pneumatic tubes; it carried letters, despatches, parcels and persons. In a word, there was no activity of either the human mind or the human hand that had not found its proper place in one or the other division of one or the other department. For each of these branches, we always found the requisite number of persons specially qualified, and properly trained for their perfect execution.

The framers of our social order demanded of every citizen an enforced service of three years in the Industrial Army, before they allowed him his choice of occupation. They thought it necessary to accustom the young man or woman to the discipline of the army, but the reader must not surmise that this discipline was a hardship or that in placing the recruits, the arbitrary will of some official decided. No violinist was ever delegated in a stone quarry, nor was a person, whose inclinations like mine, were for manual work, ever assigned to a position in a counting room; such would have been folly and would have crippled the service. As the records of every citizen were before a commission of the administration which had charge of the distribution of recruits among the various guilds, they placed each manifestation of talent into its proper place and it occurred

only in rare cases that a person decided afterwards to enter another profession, than the one
in which he had been placed at first. It was
not on Muster-day when the commissioners sent
us to our various stations, several weeks before
that day, we knew already into which department we would be enrolled. Muster-week was
more a season of enjoyment than an actual
registration for work.

. The first two days of that week belonged
to the veterans of the army, who, after a service
of thirty years, retired from work. The two
following days belonged to the so-called regulars,
who after three years of service, entered some
field of work by choice. These regulars had,
however, arrived at their decision long before,
and had filed their applications many weeks
ahead. In the Muster-week, they received
merely the ratification of their proposals. The
next two days were given to the young men
and women who entered the Army for their first
three years' service. The last day of the week
was employed in the distribution of tokens of
public acknowledgment to such as had rendered
some extraordinary service to the community.

At my time, regulars and recruits assembled
in twenty-five large cities in the land. Owing
to the increase in population, the number of

these places of assembly has been raised now to forty.

The most elaborate and complete provision was made beforehand for the reception of such a vast concourse of people in these towns. Everything was arranged in the most exact and orderly fashion. The number of guests was known to those in charge of the arrangements. and there were no surprises. Tents were erected in the suburbs of these cities for the reception of the guests assigned to them; provisions were stored up for their support, and all sanitary arrangements were perfected to avoid any danger of epidemics. In a word, everything was done to prevent accidents which are likely to happen when such vast masses of people are moved. The transportation service of the country was of course taxed to its utmost capacity, and whenever a chief of that department had succeeded so well that neither an accident nor a delay had occurred, he was sure to win the favor of the public and to receive in the following year a public recognition of some kind. No wonder, therefore, that this branch of service became perfected to the highest degree possible to human skill, intelligence and and forethought.

It happened that, with a number of class-

mates, I received orders to report for muster at
Atlantis. I say it happened, because not neces-
sarily were we always sent to the places of our
birth; it was more the exception than the rule
that we entered the army in the city in which
we were born.

Without accident, we reached Atlantis on the
day previous to the opening of the festivities.
I was assigned to a camp that was pitched near
the primary school of which I had been an
inmate, so that I was perfectly familiar with
the vicinity and made myself useful by serving
as a guide to a number of my associates who
wanted to look about the neighborhood. I at
once paid my respects to my mother whom I
had not seen for a whole year. She, as well as
her husband, gave me a most cordial welcome.
She told me of the progress my brother and
sister were making and chatted with me most
pleasantly upon the various topics of the day.

I could not refrain from speaking to her of
our mutual friend, Miss Horton, and learned that
Violet had called upon her and had told her of
our acquaintance. She was, at present, not in
the city, having been sent to enter the army at
some other recruiting place.

I could not tell precisely whether or no my
mother suspected that the high esteem which I

expressed for the young artist sprang from other sentiments than the simple appreciation of her art, but I thought she questioned me in a peculiar manner and dropped some extraordinary remarks concerning Miss Horton. She was a wonderful girl, she affirmed, and worthy of the friendship of any young man, but she doubted whether her predilections would blend with mine so that our friendship would hold out for a life time, or whether she would be able to stimulate talents such as I possessed. "After all," she said, "I should always advise a young man, who is choosing a friend of the other sex, to select one who is not of his own age. You will learn in time that we women mature more quickly, and when of equal ages, we are always your seniors. The most enduring friendships between men and women are always found between couples of which the woman is the junior by several years."

I called to renew upon new terms my relations with some of my former teachers, but to my regret, I found but few of them left in the old place. Mr. Rogers had been promoted to the position of head supervisor of all nurseries of the city. Miss Bella had married. She was mother of several children and expecting another increase in her family she had at present withdrawn from service and was not in town. The husband of Mrs. Howe had been transferred to some other school; Mrs. Howe had, therefore, also asked for a transfer to the same institution, and it had been granted. Mr. Groce, one of the veterans, was about to leave the service during the week of the Muster.

I was greatly pleased to meet two of my former schoolmates, Milton Green and Harry: Milton was to enter the army as a regular, and Harry, who was of my age, as a recruit like myself. I had not seen them for many years and hardly would have recognized them had we not happened to meet at Mr. Groce's residence.

We refreshed each other's memory in regard to our youthful days and remembered the visits we had made to the city in one another's company.

Milton had always been a great reader; he had developed into a literary man. His first three years he had served as an assistant teacher in the same primary school in which he had been reared, and he was now ready to choose that occupation for good. He had become an expert in teaching the art of reading and writing.

Harry had been brought up in schools that had developed his economic talents; he was to serve now in some branch of the distributing department. Already, his knowledge of all kinds of goods was astonishing. He could name the price of almost any article and the cost of its production.

The parade took place near the grounds on which we were encamped. Seats had been prepared upon a tract of land that was set aside for the purpose, and not less than three hundred thousand people filled the stalls of the vast amphitheatre. In the midst of the arena was erected a grand-stand upon which a delegation from the various departments took .their seats, with the mayor of the City of Atlantis, who acted as their spokesman. An orchestra of five hundred musicians rendered the music, by the strains of which the battalions passed the delegation. Each guild formed their own companies and carried their own banners, flags and insignia.

After the veterans had passed in review, they formed a circle around the stand and the mayor addressed them, expressing to them in his encomium the thanks of the community for the faithful services which they had given to it. A spokesman, elected by the veterans, answered in their behalf, promising, that whenever necessity should demand it, he, as well as all his companions, would be ready to render their services to the country for an additional year. All this, of course, is a mere matter of form ; it is repeated every year, and, therefore, creates little interest. The battalions left the grounds, amidst the cheers of the people ; flowers were thrown to them and the applause which some company received when they passed the balconies, upon which members of their guild were seated, sometimes drowned the music. The women generally received the heartiest recognition, because they had either children of their own among the audience or younger members who had been under their care in previous years, or people to whom they had rendered favors. Some men and women who, during their years of service, had lost their strength, passed in the procession on electrical vehicles, each of which carried about fifty persons. These carriages were beautifully ornamented with flowers and called forth enthusiastic cheering. Several hours were consumed by these ceremonies, after which the people returned to the city to spend the rest of the day in jollification.

The hippodromes and the theatres presented during the week their most popular productions, and the places in which the various clubs exhibited their skill in athletic sports were crowded, because special honors were offered on that public occasion to the winners. Lovers of nautical science and sports swarmed in boats of all descriptions in the harbor to witness regattas. The club-rooms of all the guilds were filled with visitors. At night the city was illuminated in a most gorgeous style and the sky ablaze with the display of pyrotechnics.

The following day was a day of rest and was spent in forming new acquaintances and renewing former friendships.

On the third day, the Regulars passed through similar exercises.

While they marched by, I detected a disparity between the number of men and women of that section. It was not alone that the columns of men were larger than those of the women, but the women were apparently older than the men, and even among themselves they differed in age by many years, some of them appearing to be nearer to thirty than to twenty-three.

How did it happen? I was puzzled.

I was never diffident in making inquiries concerning everything that was worth knowing, and so I addressed an elderly gentleman by my side and stated to him my observation. He politely gave me the desired information.

" You know," said he, " that after the three

years of enforced service, we are given the choice of an occupation. As far as men are concerned, this privilege is exercised by all, with the exception of the few, who, detained by sickness for more than a year, leave the ranks of the recruits a year later. With women, however, conditions are somewhat different. The law permits them to marry after one year's active service, that is at twenty-one. Many, nay, the majority, get married at that time, and, becoming mothers, they leave the active service for two years. When they reënter it they are obliged to step into the self-same place which they had left. Again it may happen that the duties of motherhood call them from the service; thus they will lose a number of years before the three years necessary to precede their choice of occupation are absolved. Only some of the girls prefer to serve first their three years and to marry afterwards; hence it occurs that the number of Regulars among the women on Muster-day is smaller than that of men and that most of them have reached the age of thirty when they enter the ranks of the Regulars, choosing their occupation."

I thanked him for his explanation. The riddle was solved in such a manner that I

wondered why I had not found the solution
myself.

On the fifth day the Recruits appeared
before the magistrate. That day is the most
auspicious and draws the greatest crowds.
Everybody looks with delight upon the young,
whose eagerness to enter practical work can be
read in their eyes. And when they pass in
review how beautiful their faces, blooming with
health! how erect their forms! how elastic
their step! There are no curved backs or
rounded shoulders, there are no pale cheeks,
no dim eyes, hidden behind spectacles; when
their youthful voices break out in cheers how
they rend the air!

The applause that greeted each of our companies, as we marched by, was deafening. The
older people shed tears at the sight of us, tears
of joy. In us they had a glorious promise for
the future; we young men and women were to
take up the work where it dropped from their
hands. As they had worked for us and supported us, so they could expect now to be
supported in comfort during their declining
years by us new workers.

Many remembered with joy the day when
they were recruits, but they did not look back
upon that time with regret. They felt satisfied

that they had fulfilled their promises and that they had been working or were still working for the community. Every boy or girl was to them like a child of their own. They loved them all, and their love was not vitiated by that selfishness which in previous ages was a component part of the love which parents extended to their children.

On the last day of the week, ribbons were bestowed upon those who had made themselves deserving of such honorable distinction. The reason why such a recognition was rendered to a person was always announced, so that the public could clearly see that no favoritism was possible.

After such a round of ceremonies and pleasures, all were exhausted and glad to reënter the routine of daily life.

I had received orders to remain in Atlantis. I was assigned to a sub-division of the architectural department, and was to help in building a tunnel connecting this city with the city of New York. The experience which I had gained in the Colorado mines, my general cleverness in the handling of tools, and my robust health, fitted me eminently for such work. I was placed with twenty others under the charge of an officer, whose orders we had to obey and who, in his turn, received his orders from a superior officer.

I found rooms in a block where most of my fellow-workers resided and took a bed-room and a sitting-room, the latter a luxury, which I allowed myself, because I intended to devote some of my leisure to my favorite study,— chemistry. After a few days the room looked more like a laboratory than a sitting-room.

I also supplied myself with a suit of clothes such as was prescribed for the kind of work to which I was detailed, and the next morning I reported at headquarters, for the first time, to serve my country.

CHAPTER XII.

The official time constituting a day's work, was, as it is to-day, eight hours, but it is reduced when less work is needed or when the labor is disagreeable, or finally, when the character of a task is too exhausting. Six hours constituted, therefore, a day's work for us. We reported at 8 o'clock in the morning and worked till 2 p. m., which time included a recess of thirty minutes for refreshment. At 2 o'clock, we were relieved by another gang who continued where we had left off. Five days made a week because two days out of every seven were set aside for rest. In the schools, Wednesday and Saturday were holidays; in the army, the days of rest were interchangable. Some sections would be free from work on Monday and Thursday, others on Tuesday and Friday, and some on Wednesday and Sunday. Twice in a year, once in summer and once in winter, two weeks of vacation were granted but in such a manner that not all workers of a certain department, or division, were out on a holiday together. The public work was never allowed to stop and still there was not an hour, or a day, or a week, in which a large number of people were not at leisure. Most people spent their vacation in travel; of their weekly holidays, everyone disposed according to his tastes. On such days, we would visit friends, who, like ourselves, were at leisure, or we would visit the libraries, museums or places of amusement. Some would devote their holidays either to study or to sports. There were a great many who devoted these days to certain intellectual studies which possessed a fascination for them, and assembled in public lecture halls to listen to instructors who discoursed upon a variety of topics. Every man of ability who believed that he could be of service to his fellow-citizens, by discussing any particular question or science, would ask for the use of some hall for a stated hour of a given day and announce his intention to address the public on his chosen topic. His functions were honorary; he was not allowed to neglect any of his public duties on the plea that he wished to prepare for such a discourse. His only reward consisted in the honor that was shown to him by the crowds that flocked to hear him. Speakers who could not fascinate their hearers, soon dropped out, while those who were favorites with the public and managed to keep their audiences, received on Muster-day the thanks of the community and not rarely the crimson ribbon.

These speakers covered all fields of knowledge. Some would discuss political matters, others would lay before their hearers the results of historical researches. There were those who discussed the latest inventions and there were also some who treated philosophical problems. Each of these speakers appealed to the taste of certain classes and thus they all had responsive constituencies. We would go to hear first one man, and then another, and sometimes we would listen to two or three orators on the same day.

If I were to present a picture of how I spent my weeks, it would be something like this: Dressed in my working suit, I reported a few minutes before the official hour at my place of work and as that was quite a distance from the city, and it took about ten or fifteen minutes to reach it by rail, and as the time which we spent in travel to and fro, was not deducted from the hours of work I utilized that time and perused the daily papers. Our officers then assigned a day's task to each of us. If we finished it properly before the expiration of the working day, the time saved was ours; if we did not finish the task in time, we had to stay until the work was completed. This, however, very rarely occurred, partly because no task was ever made unreasonable, or could not be completed with ease within the prescribed time, partly because there were always found some who, livelier than others, had finished their work in good season and considered it their duty to help those who were not as clever or as quick as they were.

On account of my knowledge of chemistry, I had to handle the explosives, and the danger connected with such an occupation, made my office as honorable in the same measure as it was responsible.

While at work, we would chat and converse
in a most pleasant manner; the regulars, who
had made this kind of work their profession,
would teach us youngsters every trick by which
the work could be made easy and we could
husband our forces. They would tell us also
of the experiences of their lifetime; of books
they were reading, of experiments they were
making during their leisure, of hobbies which
they rode, etc. When lunch-time arrived, a
wagon, appointed like a dining-car, drove up
and we ordered whatever we pleased, enliven-
ing the repast with interesting conversation.

Returning to my residence, I would take a
bath in the natatorium, dress, take dinner
either in the dining hall of our square or in one
of the clubs that I had joined, or occasionally
I would accompany a friend upon his invitation
to his club. Dinner over, I would either work
in my laboratory or take care of a flower-bed in
our public park, which, at my request had been
assigned to my charge or I would witness a
game of baseball, if I did not participate myself. Towards evening, I would take a ride on
my bicycle, through the streets of the city and
the suburban territory. My evenings I spent
either with friends or at concerts or at a
theatre.

My days of rest were passed in a similar manner, excepting that I remained in bed for a longer time, took my bath in the morning and attended one or two of the public lectures to which I have already referred. I was still interested in topics of the kind that had stirred up my curiosity when I was a boy, and my favorite orator was a professor who spoke upon what he called "the religions of former ages and the ethical development of the human race." It was at that time that I began reading with intense interest the lectures of my father and comparing his remarks with those of the learned professor, I became able to formulate a pretty correct picture of the time in which my father lived, also of the reasons why our present social order had so greatly surprised him.

I once called upon the professor, who expressed his delight in meeting "Young West." The rare manuscripts in my possession were a great help to him in a historical investigation which occupied him at present and of course, I loaned them to him. His opinions in regard to the past and future were about the same as those which Mr. Brandon, our teacher, had offered to us, only that I understood their exposition much better now than I did at that time. The question, however, was yet puzzling me why our ancestors needed so much and, therefore, believed so strongly in the interference of what they called, the "Divine Power" in human affairs, and why we in our days can live most happily together without resorting to all the suppositions or superstitions by which they tried to explain the order of the universe or to control the passions and vicious habits of the people. The professor thought the solution of the problem to be very simple.

"It was their misfortune," said he, "that they worked one against the other, and not one for the other. At their time society did not guarantee the existence and the ample support of every citizen; hence they needed some protector, who as they presumed, would take special interest in their little personal affairs and would stand by them in their warfare against one another. To obtain this end, they thought they must show their respect and deference to that power; hence worship and religious services were instituted. As their hopes were rarely realized, and as despite their faith and confidence in a divine protection, they were not unfrequently defeated by their human enemies and subjected to the will of the victors, they were obliged to pin their ultimate hopes to a life that was to follow their earthly career, and in which, as they supposed, all wrongs would be righted, the malefactors be punished, and the good rewarded. Both their faith in the protection of God and in immortality were the natural results, the logical consequences of a social order in which *might* gave *right*."

"How did they ever happen," quoth I, "to invent our present system of government or to institute the order of things which we enjoy to-day?"

"That is a long story to narrate," was his reply, "it took a very long time before even the predictions of the few were realized, whose logic convinced them that by working together, much better results could be reached for all than by the universal warfare in which each member of society became the enemy of his neighbor or in which the personal interests of one clashed with those of the other. They were not lacking in intelligence or understanding, not even in good will to secure happiness for all; but they had not learned how to subdue all those natural forces by the aid of which we create sufficient wealth and secure a comfortable existence for all. Think only how difficult and expensive it must have been for them to build houses and to keep them in a clean and healthy condition. Aluminum was in their time a most expensive metal, glass also was costly and not until waterfalls and the ebb and tide of the ocean were put in harness to produce electricity to be used for the purposes of heating, smelting, lighting, driving all kinds of machines, and especially in the manufacture of aluminum, could they take the first step that lead to the present development. I intended," concluded he, " to deliver a course of lectures on that subject and will be pleased to see you among the interested."

The lectures proved indeed to be highly instructive, I learned a great deal from them and so much were they valued by the public, that they were printed at the expense of the community and the author was rewarded with the crimson ribbon.

My relations to my mother and to Mr. Parkman, her husband, grew very intimate during my stay in Atlantis. Mr. Parkman was a man of a very sympathetic nature. The touch of his hand was so light that a patient whom he nursed, never felt it. His avocation as nurse had developed in him such a compassion with human suffering, that to relieve it whenever he could, afforded him the highest gratification. He was self-sacrificing and I mourned his loss as did the many who had known him when a few years later he died from an infectious disease which he had caught while nursing a patient, whose life he had saved at the expense of his own.

My sister Edith had grown up and promised to become a beautiful girl; she was at High school and her talents ran in the medical line. She became afterwards a prominent physician. Edward, my younger brother, was in an intermediate school in the neighborhood of the city, near the seashore. He showed talents and inclinations for the profession of a sailor and he ended a most remarkable and successful career as captain of a vessel.

Miss Horton still occupied my thoughts, and my infatuation was intensified by the letters which we faithfully exchanged. She had been assigned to an orchestra in one of the provincial cities on the Pacific coast. I husbanded, therefore, my allowance, in order to save the means for a trip to that city during my first vacation. I could scarcely await the time, and when it finally arrived, I secured passage upon an aeroplane. Thirty hours after rising, we descended at the place of my destination. I had not informed her of my proposed visit, intending to take her by surprise. Arriving at a late hour in the afternoon, I hastened to take a room in the nearest hotel and to secure a seat for the

concert in which I knew she was to appear.
Since I had seen her, she had improved in execution and in her interpretation of musical
works. I learned that she was a favorite in the
city and that whenever she was the soloist of
the evening, the hall was always crowded.

Her astonishment at seeing me was indeed
great and she promised to devote all her leisure
time to me in recognition of the fact that I
had travelled such a distance for the sole purpose of renewing and strengthening the friendship into which we had been drawn more than a
year ago. She introduced me to her friends,
and my pleasure in meeting these people would
have been much greater had it not been that
they would invariably ask the question: " Are
you the same " Young West" whose father was
recusitated after slumbering a whole century?"

Young West? Pshaw! I was no longer a
boy, I was a man, I worked for the community
as well as they did; what right had they to call
me Young West? I feared that this designa-
tion would tend to belittle me in the eyes of
Miss Horton.

Nevertheless, I spent a most pleasant week in
her company. We saw the sights, visited farms
and factories, and in all excursions, I was her
sole companion. I heard her in concerts and

felt proud of her successes; much more was I delighted when she played and sang for me in private. Still, there was a certain something in her conduct toward me that did not come up to my expectations. She was very kind to me; and yet that kindness differed not much from that which one might show to a perfect stranger. To tell the truth, I had expected that she would feel for me as I did for her, that she should love me because I had chanced to fall in love with her.

When I look back upon the time of my first love; when I remember the sensations which it created in my heart, I cannot help reflecting how unreasonable young people are, when they are in love. A young man meets a girl whose personal charms attract him so that he falls in love with her; at once he jumps to the conclusion, that because he has discovered her and because he loves her, she must reciprocate his feeling. Any kindness which she shows to him, he interprets at once as a token of affection and when his love remains unrequited, he finds fault not with himself but with her, and accuses her of having inspired him with false hopes, though they were all of his own creation.

I had come to visit Miss Horton without

giving her notice, without consulting even her wishes about it; she knew that the trip was expensive and that I must have denied myself many other pleasures to indulge in such an extravagance. She felt, therefore, under obligation to receive me with the greatest consideration and kindness. Would it not have been uncivil on her part had she treated me with coldness? I, however, did not place myself in her position, I had persuaded myself, that because I loved her, by necessity, she must return my love, and this, I found rather late, was a mistake.

On the day previous to my departure, I ventured to complain of the wide distance that separated me from her. "How pleasant it would be if we could pass all our leisure time in each other's company!" I said with a diffident insinuation.

"Would that not grow monotonous after a while?" she asked.

I declared that to be in her presence, to work under her eye, to counsel with her all the days of my life, would make me the happiest of men. Could she not ask for a transfer to Atlantis, or I would beg to be transferred to her city and would she be willing to marry me after the transfer was made?

Miss Horton's face first covered with crimson.

then she grew pale, but not for a moment did she lose her presence of mind or that sweetness of character which I so much admired in her.

"I must have made a grave mistake," said she, "but if I have, I beg your pardon on the ground that I made it unbeknown to myself. Your visit showed me that I must have inspired you with a strong feeling of friendship, but I did not suspect that your kindness towards me was prompted by love. I respect you as a friend; occasionally, I prefer your company to that of other men, but there are many reasons why I must decline the proposition which you have just made to me. I do not hesitate to give you my reasons for rejecting your proposal so that we may understand each other and the feeling of friendship which we have conceived for each other, be not destroyed by a misunderstanding."

"I do not intend to marry before I have entered the army as a regular; I desire to have my choice of occupation at the time when it is my privilege to choose. This is one reason for my refusal."

"My second reason is that we two are not atuned alike so that marriage could bring us that happiness which we expect of it. I want to look up to the man to whom I shall give myself body and soul, and although I admire your good qualities, I feel that I do not find my ideal in you, that I would be rather inclined to advise you than to seek counsel from you. I feel that you would look up to me and although such a thought may flatter my vanity, I am sure that such a relationship could not produce lasting happiness. That the case stands, as it does, is neither your fault nor mine; we happen to be of the same age and this alone accounts for it. The husband of my choice must be my senior by a few years and the wife that you should choose should be younger than you are. I beg you to believe me, that I esteem you too highly to offend you, nevertheless, I must tell you frankly, that as you are, you do not correspond to the ideal that I have formed of my future husband. Let us, therefore, part the friends we have been since we met, and preserve that friendship. Whenever we may meet again, let us meet as persons who understand each other thoroughly and when you will have reflected with calmness upon what I said to you, you will find that I was as much concerned in your welfare as in my own. You will find some girl more congenial to you than I can be. I hope that in time to come, you will thank me for the frankness with which I have spoken and that precisely on this account, we will become stronger friends and more reliable advisors to each other than we are now."

What could I answer her? I was not able to utter one word.

She felt deeply my embarrassment and tried, therefore, to help me overcome it. She turned the conversation gracefully upon other topics and when it was time for me to leave, she accompanied me to the aeroplane. The ship rose and she vanished from sight. With her, vanished the most pleasant dream I ever had in my life.

CHAPTER XIII.

The sting of unrequited love pains us so much more than other disappointments because it affects the most tender part of our soul, our love of self. We expect that others must love us as we love ourselves, and for no other reason than that we have chanced to fall in love with them. We forget that our passions are apt to approach us disguised in the sober vestments of friendship, and thus deceived we pretend to seek in an object of our affection the friend and not the mate. If it had been solely the friend, whom I had sought in Miss Horton, the comrade under whose eye I desired to distinguish myself, or by whose counsel I wished to profit, why did her refusal to marry me cause me so much pain? Had she refused to give me her friendship? On the other hand, if merely my passions had been inflamed by her personal charms, was she not right to doubt my assertions of love?

From the day that I had met her and had felt attracted by her talents, because they were novel to me, I had made two grave mistakes. One was, that I allowed her picture to take entire possession of my mind; the other, that I withdrew from the society of other women and thought it treason even to notice the good qualities of any of them. Had I not closed my eyes to other girls, I would have found that there were many better adapted to inspire me than was Violet, whose artistic dreams I could not have followed in any event, and that some of them were in sympathy with my plans and aspirations, yea, even looked up to me in the same manner as I did to Miss Horton. No matter how hard I tried to persuade myself that I had not been hurt by the answer which Violet made to my proposal, I was indeed sorely wounded, and for some time it gave me an indefinable, secret pleasure to keep the wound open.

However, I began to adopt a different mode of life. I ceased to dream, and one good effect of the incident which I have been describing was, that I became even more practical. If I could only succeed and distinguish myself, could I not then expect that some woman would find her ideal in me? Might not even Violet change her mind yet? She did not intend to marry for several years; there was yet some hope of winning her if only I could make myself a worthy object of her admiration.

I applied myself more diligently than ever before to my work so that my records drew the attention of my superior officers to me. Within a year I was made an officer, and appointed to take charge of a department in a factory in which high explosives were made. That such an office was given to a recruit and to so young a man as was I, was in itself an honor, because it showed that great confidence could be placed in me. The slightest neglect of duty, the slightest carelessness on my part, would have imperilled the lives of a great many. I appreciated the trust as well as the responsibilities with which it burdened me. Though my official hours of work were reduced, I gave more time to the fulfilment of my duties than the regulations required, being aware to what extent the

welfare of others was depending upon my constant watchfulness.

Also in my leisure hours, I threw myself with
greater zeal upon a series of experiments which
promised to end in some valuable discovery.
Disappointed a hundred times, I did not give up
the hope that after all I would find what I was
seeking.   Neither did I allow my official duties
nor my private studies to keep me away from
social intercourse; I sought and made many
friends among both men and women, and especially did I learn to value talents among the
latter.

My passions should not blind me a second
time.   I found that it was not absolutely necessary to enter into marital relationship to enjoy
companionship with the other sex.

My work in the factory did not require much
physical exertion and as I needed physical
exercise I sought it elsewhere.   I helped in the
labor of beautifying the parks or in any other
work in which I could make myself useful.   I
also applied myself more zealously than ever
before to gymnastics and took an active part in
all kinds of athletic sports.

When the time arrived that I should enter the
industrial army as a regular, I began to consider
seriously what occupation to choose.   Agricul-

ture had a charm for me but I was afraid it would not give me sufficient scope for my ambition. I would have liked to enter that division of the architectural department which undertook the building of roads and tunnels, but although only six hours constituted a day's work in that division, I desired to obtain still greater freedom in order to pursue my chemical experiments. I perused, therefore, carefully the official newspapers and when one day, I found that volunteers were called for to serve in the sewer division, I determined to offer my services. My application was accepted and after Muster-day, I was enrolled as a member of that section.

Our system of sewerage had reached a very high degree of perfection. It had received the most careful consideration and no efforts had been spared to increase its excellence, because the health of the whole community depended upon it. Through large tunnels, into which pipes led from every house, all foul matter was carried either far into the sea from the cities near the coast, or into the large rivers, from the cities of the interior. Whenever the tides could be utilized to work the drains automatically, they were drawn into such service while in the interior pumps, worked by electrical power, were applied. Streams of electrified water were injected not alone to wash away every particle of unclean matter, but to destroy also every infectious germ.

Our division was employed in keeping this vast system of drainage, composed of thousands of miles of pipes and tunnels in good working order, also to augment the network wherever it was needed. Our guild in the city of Atlantis numbered more than five thousand persons and the service was so well organized that even a slight flaw in it would be at once detected and remedied.

We were subdivided into a number of sections; we had our engineers, our chemists, our tunnel-builders, our inspectors, etc. Each company stood under an officer whose duty it was to see that none of the men neglected his work. These officers of the various companies reported to a commission that supervised them. Inasmuch as the sewers of the different cities of a province stood in close connection with one another, the chairmen of these commissions reported to a provincial board, and these officers, in their turn, received orders from the head of the division, who as a member of the national administration was equal in rank with the heads of the other divisions that composed the department of architecture. The companies

into which the force of men, assigned to every
city, was divided, were not equally strong in
numbers; there were fewer engineers needed
than builders; fewer were employed in the
pumping stations than in overlooking the drains.
Each company, large or small, was, nevertheless
cut up in fifteen squads, in order that the
service might run without interruption and that
no member should be obliged to work for more
than four hours a day. This sub-division provided also for two days of rest out of seven, and
besides for a vacation of four weeks in a year to
be enjoyed either at one time, or twice, of a
fortnight's duration. It allowed in addition for
absence on account of sickness.

When I entered this new field of occupation,
I was placed, as is the custom, at the lowest
round of the ladder; I became a roundsman. I
had to acquaint myself with the situation of all
the drains and the methods by which a defect
was to be discovered. I was then promoted to
the next grade and being quick to observe and
to learn, I rose from step to step, filled various
positions as officer, and after five years of service, I found myself appointed to the office of
superintendent of the sewerage of Atlantis.

As such, I served for ten years. I will not
tire the reader narrating to him all the little

incidents of my official career, I may, however,
state without any lack of modesty, that whenever I was promoted, such was not alone a
mark of recognition of faithful services rendered,
but it was also due to the recommendations of
my companions. Mine was the happy disposition to make myself liked by all men with
whom I was associated. I helped them wherever
I found them lacking, and as an officer I always
considered it my duty to help bear the burden
of those who were under my charge. They
never found me unwilling to do the same work
that I would order them to do. If a task was of
a dangerous nature, they found me ready to
lead them, and even during the years of my
superintendentship, I was seen many a time
swinging the pickaxe, handling a shovel, setting
off an explosive or whatever work was to be
done by some one in the exigency of the
moment. Moreover, whenever the hours of
official duty were passed, I treated my fellow-
workers as friends; the recruit or regular,
who had served but one day, was treated by
me like the veteran in service, and while I
required the strictest obedience during the
hours of work, in private life, I ignored all official differences. It would have been bad form
to carry official life into private life. We

respected a man for his faithful application to work, for his intelligence, for the neatness with which he completed a task and for his cheerful willingness to do more than was his duty or to take upon himself a task which one of his co-workers, on account of conditions which he was unable to control, could not fulfill.

I did not remain a bachelor, partly because I craved the companionship of the other sex, partly because public opinion considered it disgraceful to remain unmarried. We believed it to be one of the duties of good citizenship to increase the population, and both men and women who did not marry during the years when it was proper to seek an alliance, were looked upon with distrust.

I am glad to say that this healthy sentiment has not abated and the fear that conditions as they prevailed during my father's time, would return, does not trouble us. From his lectures, I learned, that at his time a great many people preferred to remain single for fear that they would not be able to support their children or to rear them in a proper manner.

I found a worthy companion among the other sex, one who brightened my life with the sunshine of her affection, who became a source of inspiration to me and who stimulated me to work for the noblest ends. Do not imagine, fair reader, that I succeeded in winning, after all, the object of my first love; no, Miss Horton had found her ideal in a fellow-artist; she had married a sculptor. I found my wife, or rather, she found me, in a way that was not at all romantic.

During the time in which I served as an officer of inferior rank, in one of the sections of my division, it was a part of my duties to order the supplies required in the service by our division. The chemicals, mostly disinfectants, the tools, the rubber suits, with which the men were furnished at public expense, we had to order from the national stores and they were properly debited to our department. Almost every day, I had, therefore, to call at the supply office, enter our orders and give receipts for goods delivered. I met·here a young woman who had just entered the service as a recruit. Emily Warren was not a total stranger to me; I had met her before in the same intermediate school of which my sister Edith was a graduate. She had shown literary talents similar to those of my sister, but while Edith's gifts landed her in the medical profession, Emily's gifts indicated administrative abilities. She graduated later from a high school and from a college in which her peculiar talents had been developed and as was expected, she was assigned to one of the many bureaus, established for the transaction of the national business. Her hours of daily work were eight, because her work was not exhausting; she had to keep certain books and to send all the requisitions filed by the various departments to a clerk whose duty it was to execute them.

She resided not very far from where I had taken rooms and as my hours of duty fell in the latter part of the day, and I made it a practice to file my orders on my way home, it happened sometimes that after receiving and entering my papers, she would leave her desk and walk home with me. Our companionship soon developed into the most cordial friendship, and our accidental walks soon became a custom; I called for her every evening to see her home.

As we had the same days of rest, it gave me exceeding pleasure to accompany her to lectures that interested her. Well versed in literature, she kept herself posted on all the latest literary productions. She was besides a brilliant conversationalist and had a way of imparting knowledge without assuming the appearance of an instructor. Many a time would she drop hints how I could facilitate my work by bring-

ing system into it, and whenever I made use of
such advice, I found that she was right and that
I succeeded so much the better for having
followed it. Her interest in my chemical experiments was so great that she would stand for
hours by my side in my laboratory, watching
my efforts, occasionally offering a suggestion
how a thing might be done more expeditiously.
Also in other respects, I found her of great
help to me ; she understood better than I did
how to select in the sample rooms the articles
which are needed for personal comfort, and thus
she would advise me what grade of cloth would
be most suitable for me, or what style and shade
would be most becoming to me. I had learned
to manage my expenditures in such a manner
that I never overdrew my accounts, and quite
to the contrary, would return to the treasury at
the end of every half year an unexpended amount,
but I was not an expert in managing my affairs
in such a manner as to be able to indulge in a
luxury without sacrificing some comfort in
another quarter. She had a way of striking
the right balance and not unfrequently would she
thus help me working out my estimates. I discovered, that, whenever she ordered a dinner
from a bill of fare, I received a better meal at
less expense than when I ordered it myself. I

made it, therefore, a practice to take my dinners
with her at the same place and at the same
hour, whenever that was possible.

When once I spent my vacation travelling,
strange to say, I felt that I missed her company. I did not enjoy that trip as I did previous ones and when my time to recuperate again
approached, I told her I should not leave the
city but would rather spend my vacation at
home, unless she could arrange to accompany
me. The idea of proposing marriage to her had
many times risen in my mind, but my former
experience had made me somewhat timid and
over-cautious She had not yet entered the
army as a regular; would she not, like Violet,
object to marital connections before that time?

One evening we took a spin on our wheels
through the suburbs and rested for a while on a
bench in one of the large parks that girded the
city. The time for my vacation was again
approaching and the conversation turned upon
my plans. She could not go with me. Her
turn came a few weeks later and she had not
yet found anyone who was ready to exchange
with her.

"Is it not rather a foolish notion of yours,
said she, to imagine you could not enjoy yourself without me? What am I to you? We

have been friends for some time, and good friends at that, but will the time not come when we will be separated for more than two weeks, maybe forever?"

I felt irritated and, with a slight touch of anger in my voice, I said: "It seems that you could miss my company without discomfort; for all I know, you may be glad to get rid of me for a fortnight!"

She looked at me with astonishment, and after a pause, she asked: "Do you yourself believe what you have said just now? You do know that I will miss you, and why should I deny it? I dread the time of your absence. Let us come to an understanding. I have been aware for quite a time that I have found in you a congenial companion in whom I could place my fullest confidence and trust, and quite frequently I have questioned myself whether separation would not cast a shadow over my life. If, then, it is true that you cannot enjoy yourself for two weeks without me, would it not be advisable for us to make a covenant of friendship that would last forever?"

"And do you indeed love me enough to become my wife?" cried I; "may I assume that you think me the ideal companion, which, as I am aware, every woman is seeking?"

She did not answer, but blushingly she hid her head on my breast. I threw my arms around her and a kiss sealed the contract, which, afterwards concluded, I have never for one moment repented. We arose from our seats, and, returning to the city, we discussed the particulars of our prospective union.

The very next day we went to the registration office. The degree of relationship in which a couple who wished to get married might possibly stand was to be first ascertained, to prevent alliances between too near relatives. We were not even distantly related and a license was granted. Our marriage intentions were published and my vacation was to be our honeymoon.

We invited a small number of friends and our nearest relatives to witness the final ceremonies of registration. At the appointed hour, we all met at the office; Emily and I made our declarations, and we were pronounced man and wife by the registering clerk.

Our friends rendered their felicitations to us and a repast, which we partook with our guests in the club-room of my guild, increased this day's happiness. My wife had previously resigned her lodgings, and I had managed to secure rooms for her adjoining to mine. Her parents, who resided in a neighboring city, had come to witness the ceremonies, and her mother, as well as mine, introduced Emily into her new quarters.

CHAPTER XIV.

The novelists of the mediæval times, as far as the twentieth century, were in the habit of describing the adventures, fortunes, and misfortunes of some young man or woman until they had brought their hero or heroine safely into the bridal chamber. That event closed their story, as if marriage, in fact, had ended all, and as if the life of a noble, ambitious and enterprising person became so insipid after marriage that it could offer no further incident worthy to be narrated. How queer! From my own experience, and from that of my many friends whom I have consulted in the matter, I have learned that the real life of a man begins after marriage, and that the years preceding it are merely preparatory to it. How insignificant is all that I did or experienced previous to my marriage, when I compare it with the aspirations and ambitions which filled my soul after I had become a husband and a father! My efforts had so far been aimless; now, I did all for a settled purpose. The union with a partner chosen from the other sex had completed my being and rounded all my activities. If I ever had been careful in my work, if I ever had fulfilled a task assigned to me with promptness and accuracy, now I was still more careful and my zeal for work increased. I had been ambitious, I had been proud of whatever honorable distinction was conferred upon me; the studies which I had pursued had been undertaken in the hope of winning further honors; but I owe it to my wife, to her inspiration as well as to her coöperation, that I began to reach after the ultimate goal, toward which the eye of every ambitious citizen is directed, namely,— the presidency. Marriage had made a man of me; it had awakened in me a new and higher consciousness.

My wife was indeed a friend, a companion, a counsellor to me. We easily arranged so to exchange with others that our hours of leisure, our days of rest, and our vacations coincided. What happy hours we passed when we returned from work! We would study together; her taste for literary pursuits remained not without influence upon me; she introduced me somewhat into the great world of thought in which I had been a stranger heretofore. My inclinations for practical work, on the other hand, brought my wife back to the realities of life whenever her dreams would carry her too far.

She would give to my reports a polish which made them interesting reading, dry as were sometimes the facts of which they treated, and thus the attention of my superiors was drawn to them. "What a brilliant writer Young West has grown to be," one of the commissioners under whom I stood would say; "it breaks the monotony of my work to read his reports; compared with the rest, they are refreshing; they are like an oasis in the desert; one would hardly believe that he is the author; he is such a matter-of-fact man." Thus most of my promotions were due to this aid which Emily afforded me.

Our marital felicity was increased, when, one day, she whispered into my ear that she expected to become a mother; and two months later she sought the release from service to which her condition entitled her.

Motherhood is highly honored by us and the nation does not begrudge a woman her support during the time in which she withdraws from the army in order to devote herself to the holiest of all her obligations, to give to the community citizens who will take up the work where it must pass from our hands.

Relieved from all care, my wife devoted now her whole attention to the duties which a mother owes to a child in its prenatal state. She turned her mind to the noblest thoughts and advanced the healthful development of the yet unborn by appropriate physical exercises. She would visit the museums and study the features and forms of statues or pictures that the highest art had produced.

The last few weeks were weeks of anxiety to me. In expectation of the coming event, she had secured a room in one of the hospitals appointed and arranged for these daily occurrences. The rules of this institution permitted me to see her only once a day, and then only for a short time.

One morning, I was notified by despatch that I had a son. My heart was thrilled with joy; I hastened to see mother and child, who were both doing well. He was a beautiful child, sound and strong; at least we believed there was never another child born like him. After a few weeks, Emily returned to her rooms to devote her care solely to the physical development of her babe. The small additional expenditures which the support of a child demanded, were covered by the usual allowance which the nation sets aside for every child. The birth had been registered by the hospital authorities, and as we had agreed beforehand upon a name in case the child should be a boy, he was entered in the records as " Leete West," in memory of my grandfather.

I received many congratulations from my friends and the only disagreeable feature of these days of joy was that they would talk in the clubs of the news that " Young West had been presented by his wife with a boy!" or " What a happy man Young West is since he has become a father;" or "It was quite appropriate that Young West should name his boy after his grandfather." Always and ever "Young West!" My wife laughed whenever I felt irritated by that nickname and said that she preferred me to be " Young West." When she agreed to marry me, she said she was well aware that she married " Young West," and as long as she did not find fault with the name, why should I?

A babe is an amusing toy; a kind of plaything for the diversion of parents. We enjoyed playing with the child and watching the gradual awakening of his consciousness. His first smile delighted us; when he cut his first tooth, we felt proud ; when he made the first attempts to walk, we invited our friends to behold the wonder.

The time, however, came when we observed that excepting the instinct which teaches every living being how to rear its young ones, we did not possess sufficient knowledge to develop the child physically and mentally in a rational, systematic manner. We reproached ourselves for being over-indulgent with him, and we began to fear that we might do him more harm by our affection than good. Therefore, at the proper time, we brought him to the nursery of our square.

In one of his lectures, my father informed his audience that in his days the care of children was left entirely to the parents; that besides their daily work they had to attend to them, no matter whether they had made a study of child nature or not, and that it would have been considered a cruelty to take a child away from his parents. "Only in the most ancient times," he said, "did a state flourish in Greece that considered the child the property of the commonwealth and removed it from parental influences ; but," he continued, "the civilization of my days would have been shocked at such an interference with parental rights."

How queer all that sounds! If a couple
could now be found who would wish to assume
the grave responsibilities and undertake to educate their children, the nation would gladly
grant them permission to do so; but it is
because we love our children so well that we
give them in charge of persons who have made
a study of child nature and hence are competent
to develop them properly, letting alone that
parental instincts blind them to their evil traits.
How can one remove a defect if he does not see
it? How could I have been expected to unfold
my child's mind when I understood absolutely
nothing about education? My judgment was
good in my line of work, I could advise how to
build a tunnel, how to set off an explosive. I
was familar with the construction of a pump, I
knew how to divide a certain task among a
number of men, but I knew nothing about the
treatment of a child, nothing about the food
that was best for him, nothing about exercises
that would best develop his physical system.
Or, how could we have found the time to watch
the child? Even if we would have given all
our leisure hours to our boy, who would have
looked after him while we were at work? It
seems to me that it was selfish in the highest
degree to deny to a child the intelligent education

which the country alone can give the young citizen, for no other reason than that it pleases a parent to toy with his child and to be amused by his youthful pranks. The fact of parenthood does not give us the right to interfere with the real welfare of a child. Again, I repeat it, because we do love our children we entrust them to the care of talented educators, and we spare no efforts to make our educational institutions, the lowest as well as the highest, as perfect as we can possibly make them.

I passed through the same parental experiences five times. We had three boys in all, and two girls.

In the meantime two things happened to foreshadow the most important events in my life. One was that I received promotion into the board of commissioners who superintended the whole provincial system of sewerage, and that after two years of service I was chosen by my colleagues to act as their chairman, which office placed me at the head of the division. The other was that my researches and experiments were finally crowned with success. I had discovered a chemical process by which offal could be not only deodorized, but which would destroy also every infectious germ contained therein. I had been led to these studies and experiments almost by accident.

During my years of education in the high school and the college, I had been sent at various times to large farms, on account of my love for agricultural labors, and it was there that I observed how the land failed many a time to give proper returns, lacking proper fertilization. Chemical compounds were used, it is true, to stimulate the soil, but never was returned to the acre fully what had been taken from it. It also happened accidentally that, reading one of my father's lectures, I learned that one of the great chemists of his time had made a similar observation. I searched the libraries for his works, found them, studied them and became more strongly convinced that in course of time the productive forces of the earth must become exhausted unless we return to the land every year as much as we draw from it.

We had taken a great deal of pride in our system of sewerage ; we had perfected it during the last half century to such a degree that it became almost impossible to further improve it. It had indeed answered all purposes. It had saved labor and prevented sicknesses. One important thing, however, was overlooked. Our large cities sent annually to the unfathomable depths of the ocean the very strength of the earth, the very material out of which nature produces our support.

How could this waste be prevented? How could the refuse that accumulated in our vast centres of population be returned to the ground from which it originally came, without imposing unpleasant tasks upon a number of citizens, or exposing the community to the dangers of infectious diseases?

This was the problem which I undertook to solve, and after years of patient labor, after many disappointments, which sometimes discouraged me to such an extent that I was inclined to drop the whole matter in despair, I finally succeeded, thanks to the encouragement of my wife, who would always tell me not to give up but to try again.

I began now to write a series of articles setting forth my discoveries and showing how they could be applied advantageously. When I say I began to write these essays, I utter but a half-truth; I supplied merely the arguments, the facts, the professional terms, while my wife wrote the composition in the lucid and interesting style of which she was master.

These publications created quite a sensation.

They had appeared originally in a periodical of
our guild, but they were at once copied by the
agriculturists, chemists, and all such departments
as were professionally interested in them.
They met, however, with greater opposition
than I expected, and capable writers undertook
to answer my arguments. Thus a fierce contro-
versy arose. Some would accept my suggestions in part; others would throw them aside *in
toto* as Utopian. Some would praise " Young
West "' for his sagacity and foresight, others
would roundly denounce " Young West." as a
schemer — as one who, to gratify his ambition,
would impose upon the country an effort which
would call every citizen into service for an
additional term.

" We have," they said, " just finished a work,
grander than any which the history of mankind
records; we have built a network of drains
such as the world had never seen ; we have
abolished that class of unpleasant work which,
in former centuries, had made slavery a necessity; we have done away with most epidemics
and thus increased the average length of human
life by a good number of years ; and now comes
" Young West " and proposes to abandon the
whole system, to fill up the drains, to build new
reservoirs for the reception of refuse matter, to

establish a new service for transformation of that matter into a fertilizer. He tells us that his chemical composition will deodorize all ex- crements, that it will destroy infectious germs, but is he sure that what may be practicable in the laboratory will be as practicable when applied to the immense masses of disintegrating matter which it will have to treat? One epi- demic which his experiment might cause, would cost the lives, perhaps, of millions. Is the nation ready for such an experiment? — for such a possible sacrifice? And what is the good that we are assured that we shall derive from it? He fears that in a couple of hundred years the earth will cease to bring forth fruit, and thus human life will be imperilled. We will admit that it is our duty to prepare for future emergencies, but are his fears justified? Are they not rather far-fetched and absurd? Are not the historical records full of such or similar predictions which never came to pass? Have not innumerable scientific theorists prophe- sied that in the end the earth would cool· off to such an extent that all vegetation and with it animal existence would be made impossible, but have their predictions ever come true? When the stores of coal began to be exhausted, and people became afraid that civilization would come to an end, did they not learn how to produce electricity without the aid of coal, so that, instead of being retarded, civilization advanced?"

All the divisions of the architectural department, except the sewerage battalion, were loud in their denunciations of " Young West's absurdities," as they called them. The divisions of the agricultural department, on the other hand, who observed the falling off of the earth's fertility, stood by me, their periodicals took up my defence and insisted that the experiment was at least worth trying.

For a number of years, the battle thus raged in the monthly magazines of the various guilds. During vacation weeks I would travel to other cities, especially in the agricultural districts, and exhibit models of the new plant, or explain my discovery. I asked for no more than to be permitted to transform the offal of only one city into a fertilizer and to return it to a given area of land, to prove by the results the correctness of my deductions and the feasibility of my plans.

Progress, however, was slow; my scheme had more opponents than supporters ; people feared that the introduction of my system would increase not alone the daily hours of work, but would necessitate the draft of veterans at least for one year's extra service. Such a draft had been made but once, and, strange to say, in order to institute the present system of sewerage to which I was so much opposed.

Many times did I determine to give up the struggle, to do my duty as a plain citizen and to leave well-enough alone; but it was due to my wife's exhortations and encouragement that I held out and remained steadfast. She prophesied final success; she held out before me the honor of the blue ribbon. Would she not feel proud of her husband? Would it not have an influence upon our children, as well as upon all the young, to see persistency rewarded? Was not the respectful and grateful rememberance of posterity immortality indeed for which all should strive?

At last the wind began to shift; some straws began to show that it was turning and that public opinion commenced to change in favor of my plans.

CHAPTER XV.

The narrative of my presidential campaign might become unintelligible to readers of a later century unless I embodied in this book for their special benefit a description of the methods with which the nations in our day govern themselves. Will my contemporaries, therefore, kindly pardon me when I present in the following chapter a picture of our political machinery with which they, of course, are familiar?

Self-government was the glorious ideal after which the nations of old were constantly reaching, although this phantom escaped their embrace every time when they thought they had captured it. Wearied by despotism, tired of monarchy, they believed that a republic would indeed secure for them what they desired, viz.: a government of the people, for the people, and by the people. After a brief experience they found to their sorrow that these hopes, too, were delusive. Instead of by one monarch or one despot they were now ruled by hundreds of political bosses, or by moneyed corporations, syndicates and monopolies too numerous to be counted. The very representatives whom they elected to transact the public business betrayed them, and the iron hand of despotic majorities rested more heavily upon them than had in previous ages the hand of an irresponsible tyrant.

In vain they tried to reach the will of the sovereign people. Let alone that political equality can not exist unless social and economical equality support it, their axiom, that the " majority must rule," was a fallacy, if not in itself at least in its execution. Given a community of a hundred people, was it right that, fifty-one voting for one measure and forty-nine for another, the latter should be made subservient to the former? Or was it indeed the " vox populi," the voice of the sovereign people that was heard when in a three cornered contest the party which cast thirty-six ballots was allowed to prescribe laws to the remaining sixty-four? Small wonder, therefore, that the people at my father's time continuously tinkered their election laws, and that, no matter how shrewdly they meandered their election districts, or how ingeniously they constructed their automatic ballot boxes, the cunning found always a way to defeat the public will.

Finally the honest and thinking classes came

to the conclusion that their whole system of electing a government was a failure and a farce ; they objected to serve any longer as voting-cattle and to hurrah for some scheming politician, who, by shrewd machinations or by the depth of his bar'l, had succeeded in capturing a nomination. Elections had then come to serve as a popular pastime. There were municipal elections every year; state elections every second year; national elections every fourth year. Half a year previous to these elections, the opposing parties and their candidates would begin to abuse each other to the best of their ability, and the partisans would stake large sums of money upon the success of their favorites, precisely as they would upon a favorite race-horse. The economic interests of the country, on the other hand, became paralyzed during the time, if they were not killed outright. Who cared ?

When the social order which we enjoy at present hove in sight, its framers evolved a constitution so different from that of their ancestors that a great many of their supporters even doubted its feasibility, and feared that instead of enhancing liberty it would destory it, because the new order went almost to the extreme and reduced what was formerly called " the expression of the public will," "the safeguard of liberty," to a minimum. That they had not been mistaken, that they had discovered at last the most effective method of good government, is known to us, and although our children may yet improve certain details, it is our hope that in its main features the constitution of our days will be able to satisfy in its execution the remotest generations.

It now became the duty of the government to marshal the members of the nation in their common fight against hunger, cold, disease and ignorance; its functions were, therefore, others than they had been before, and were divided among the number of departments of which I had occasion to speak in a previous chapter. To make these various offices elective would have been absurd. What, for example, does an agriculturists know of the needs of the architectural department, or can he tell whether a person is qualified for any of its offices? Every department appointed, therefore, its own officers according to fitness. Every officer was now made the servant of the people in the true sense of the word; he received no extra remuneration, and for the honor which the office conferred upon him he dearly paid by the responsibilities with which it burdened him. The commis-

sioners, who appointed the officers, were generally led in their decisions both by the records
of a candidate and by the recommendations of
his co-workers. Inasmuch as the ranks of the
higher officials were filled by promotions from
the next lower rank, no person ever occupied a
higher position unless he had become thoroughly familiar with the duties of all the
inferior offices and had faithfully served a term
in them. A person who eventually entered the
cabinet as the head of a department had passed
through all the offices below it; he had even
served as a private. The president, whose pre-
rogative it was to select among the aspirants
the best qualified for a cabinet office, in place of
the members who went out of service, could
make no grave mistakes, and could be sure in
almost every case that the men appointed by
him were thoroughly conversant with the
minutest details of the work which their departments had to cover, because he could choose
only from those who were serving in a position
next to that of a cabinet officer.

The heads of the divisions in every department formed at the same time a board, whose
duty it was to legislate for the proper conduct
of business in their branch; also to arbitrate
whenever a difference arose between sections.

If, as it sometimes happened, two departments came in conflict with one another, each of the contesting parties would select the head of another department, and these two arbitrators would choose a third one, form a court, listen to the evidences, and decide who was right or wrong. Their verdict was final and the contesting parties had to yield.

The president only was chosen directly by the people, that is by the veterans, to whom alone had been given the privilege of the ballot. After a faithful service of thirty years they were trusted to know what the country needed and to what rights their guilds were entitled. Being interested in every public question, only in so far as the welfare of the whole country guaranteed also their own, they entered upon a political campaign without passion or bias.

Candidates for this highest of all offices could be chosen solely from the small number of men or women who had served in the cabinet as heads of a department or of a division, and who had retired from public service for at least five years.

The election of a president never turned around a person: its pivot was always some principle. Whenever some new, great, public work was to be undertaken, to whom could it be entrusted more safely than to a person who was specially qualified to carry it out? If it fell into the architectural line, an architect was made president; if it fell into the department of electricity, an electrician was raised to that office, etc. At every presidential campaign the question was not what person was to govern the country, but what work was the most desirable to be performed at the time. It was in this field of discussion that parties clashed with one another; some would be honestly of opinion that one kind of work was more needed than another and ought to receive preference; others would claim as honestly that another enterprise was deserving of first attention.

Each class of work was thus represented by a presidential candidate, and the election took place in the following manner.

Every veteran of a guild had the right of his own opinion in regard to one or the other proposed measures, and was, therefore, allowed to cast his ballot for the candidate of his choice. The nominee who received the majority vote of a department was made its candidate, and the one who carried the greatest number of departments became president. This method of election had found favor, because the interests of all the members of a guild were identical, and a majority vote of them represented in a general way the sentiment of their department. The wish of the greatest number of departments stood then for the will of the whole people, or came at least as near to it as it was possible to ascertain.

I will now return to my story, presuming that my prospective readers understand the situation.

After my articles had directed the attention of the country to my discovery, and after my plans had been discussed in all their aspects for a number of years in the public prints, people began to see that there was some truth at least in my statements and some logic at least in my arguments. Some periodicals, therefore, advocated a trial. The agriculturists were the more eager to ascertain whether my projects were feasible, as the crops had been poor during the last few years, and the force as well as the hours of labor in the fishery divisions had to be increased in order to make good the deficiency. The country had not yet suffered, but as many preferred a vegetarian diet to meat or fish, that class had been greatly inconvenienced by the partial failure of the cereal supply. The people found thus that something should be done to improve agriculture, and most wisely they agreed upon the election of an agriculturist to the presidential office. When Mr. Rust, who had served at the head of the agricultural department, was nominated for the office, no dissenting voice was heard. The campaign was a tame one, and his election was almost a unanimous one.

The new president had known me for many years in my official capacity as superintendent of the sewers of Atlantis. He had not only read my articles, but had given me a chance to explain them in person to him, at which occasion I had found him an enthusiastic listener. After he had left the service, he had travelled for a number of years in foreign countries, where, I suppose, he must have made observations that strengthened him in his convictions that I was right, and that no matter how great the expense would be to establish plants, as I proposed them, the country would enormously gain in the end.

No sooner was he installed in his office than he induced the chief of the architectural department to offer to me the vacant position of head of the whole division of sewerage, which office entitled me to a seat in the cabinet.

Owing to her duties of motherhood, my wife had entered the regulars at rather an advanced age. That she might stay in Atlantis with me, she had chosen the same work in the supply department, in which she had been employed before. She was more ambitious than I, and yet she preferred to gratify her ambition rather indirectly through me than directly through aspiring for a more prominent position for herself.

"It is immaterial to mè," she would say, "whether I serve the community by my own work or by aiding you in your efforts. In the end it is the same. If I were to carve out for myself a sphere of action which would bring me more prominently before the country I could not assist you in your greater work, and my vanity would do more harm than good. Let me work with you ; I will be satisfied with whatever rays of glory will fall upon me from the renown and the immortal fame that will shine upon you."

On her account I hesitated, therefore, to accept the honorable office that was offered to me ; not for all the fame in the world, would I have parted from her for a year, and not until a suitable position in the capital was found for my wife did I accept.

I had now dwelt and labored for a quarter of a century in the city of my birth. For three years I had served as a recruit, for five years as

a private and subaltern officer in the sewerage
service; during ten years I superintended the
whole section; for two years I was a member
of the provincial board, and during five years I
was their chairman. This made in all twenty-
five years.

In the meantime some of my children had
grown up; Leete was in his last collegiate year
and intended to enter the manufacturing department. My two other boys were in the
high and intermediate schools; so was one of
my daughters; the youngest was yet an inmate
of the primary.

My mother, a widow for the second time, had
left the service many years ago and was at
present travelling in a warmer climate for the
sake of her health.

I had a large circle of friends, and so had my
wife. We were well liked in the clubs to
which we belonged, and now that we were to
leave the city they desired to give us a token
of the esteem and love in which we were held
by them.

Two days previous to our departure one of
my friends called and proposed that we should
meet him the next day at a given hour, to take
dinner with him at one of our club rooms. We
accepted; but great was our surprise when we

found that more than a hundred persons had assembled to dine with us at the same time. A committee had prepared quite an elaborate pro- gramme of postprandial exercises. Artists had been invited to entertain us with song and instru- mental music. In verse and in prose, the regret was expressed by the guests that they should lose us, coupled, however, with congratulations and well wishes for our future. The company was composed of members from all departments, of officers as well as of privates; there were men and women, veterans, regulars, and even re- cruits. A photographer took a flash-light picture of the scene, and each of the guests pre- sent afterwards received a copy of it by which to remember the farewell banquet rendered to "Young West and his wife by his many friends."

With the exception of the most necessary arti- cles of the wardrobe, we returned our modest furniture to the stock-rooms of Atlantis, and received an order for a supply similar to it, to be taken from the national storehouse of the city to which we had been transferred.

The next day we left Atlantis by aeroplane and arrived safely at our destination. Friends had secured rooms for us in advance. We furnished them, and, having attended to our personal comforts, we reported ourselves ready for work, I in the cabinet, my wife in the supply department.

CHAPTER XVI.

It had been frequently proposed, and once a hot and closely contested campaign had been fought on account of it, that the seat of our government should be transferred to a part of the country that was more centrally located than the District of Columbia. The people of South America, even of Mexico and California, complained bitterly that the national capital was at too great a distance from their provinces, and that their delegates were compelled to travel sometimes two days and two nights to reach Washington.

However, the hardship of a prolonged travel was not deemed sufficient reason to abandon a city which had become identified with the administration of the land, or to give up the buildings which had been especially erected during the last two centuries, at enormous expense, for the proper transaction of the national business.

Washington had grown and had become a city of enormous size. It counted nearly two

millions of inhabitants, most all of them employed in either purely administrative work or in
supplying the needs of this great army of officials. Of manufacturing establishments there
were none to be found, neither in the city nor
in its nearest neighborhood. Some of the
citizens were employed in horticulture, but the
products of their gardens were barely sufficient
to supply the demands of the city, and the
national markets were stocked with the surplus
of the provinces.

Washington was built like the rest of our
cities. Its private residences did not differ from
the ones I had seen elsewhere; its hospitals,
schools, sample-rooms, and storehouses were like
those in Atlantis or New York. If the city
owned a feature which distinguished it from
other centres of population it was that it
possessed a larger number of hotels than any
other city upon the continent to accommodate
both the visiting delegates that flocked to the
seat of government from all parts of the country to transact their business, and the pleasure-
seeking public who, during vacation time, would
come to inspect the wonders of the national
capital. The museums, libraries and art galleries of the city were indeed wonders of architecture. The greatest glory to which a painter

or a sculptor aspired was to have one of his
works admitted into the national galleries, or
even placed as an ornament in any of the
government buildings.

Most of the typesettiug and printing business
was done right here. The " National News
Register " was edited in the city; circulating
throughout the length and breadth of the country, it employed more than ten thousand people
to issue its sheets. The division which was in
charge of the accounts which the nation kept
with every individual covered acres of land.
Thousands of people were kept busy in the
manufacture of subscription blanks, and if the
system of the governmental machinery had not
been so well devised a much greater number of
people would have been needed to attend to this
department of the administration alone.

A position in Washington was not a sinecure.
In the same degree as it was honorable, it drew
upon the time and the energy of the incumbent.
The daily hours of service were nominally eight,
but the higher his position the more did an
officer feel obliged to give a part of his leisure
to his work. The majority of the members of
the government were of my age, i. e., about
forty-five years old, the very time in life when

a person finds his highest satisfaction in work and cares less for enjoyments.

The social atmosphere of the city was very enjoyable, because the highest talents which the land produced were concentrated in this place. The people of Washington represented, so to say, the flower of the country. One could not walk in the streets for five minutes without meeting a man or woman who wore the white, crimson, green, or blue ribbon; i. e., who had distinguished themselves in some sphere of activity.

My labors were more arduous than I had imagined them to be. Of course I did not work with my hands, nor had I to inspect the details of given tasks, but I had to pass judgment upon the reports which came from every bureau under me, and as a mistake on my part would have been followed by grave consequences, I had to be very careful. I had also to travel extensively, but after a man has satisfied his curiosity, travelling ceases to be a pleasure to him. Many a time did I regret having accepted my position, and many a time did I look back with envy upon the happy days when I worked as a private for only four hours a day in the sewers of Atlantis and had ample time to pursue my studies or to enjoy the company of my wife. Had it not been for her encouraging words, I should have resigned my office and begged to be returned to a position of less responsibility.

" Every citizen," said she, " must do his best for his country. If the ones who are able to lead others, will refuse to do their share of the public business because the work is too onerous for them or the responsibilities too great, how can the country ever prosper, or who is to take their places? The country has done for you all in her power, has she not the right to ask of you to do your very·best for her? Besides, the blue ribbon is now within your reach; your grandfather wore it, why should not you? May not, after all, the highest office in the gift of the country be offered to you? Would you give up all aspirations for the only true immortality simply because you must devote a few more hours to your work than seems to be compatible with your convenience and your personal comfort? "

After such conversations, I generally went to work with renewed vigor.

One of the first acts of President Rust was to convene a conference of all the members of his cabinet, to discuss the pros and cons of the plans and schemes which I had proposed in my articles. For more than three weeks we studied the question, and as I had a chance to explain by word of mouth the details of my discovery, I made many converts of people who had been seriously opposed to them. The conference finally agreed to make a trial on a small scale and under restrictions which would prevent any possible danger to the public or any unnecessary waste of energy. The departments most interested in my schemes would be asked to carry the greatest burden of my experiment, which was not more than right. Two calls were therefore issued: one to cities who would volunteer to have provisional plants established in their midst for the transformation of refuse matter into a fertilizer ; the other, to veterans, willing to serve an additional year for the purpose of building a plant after my designs."

In the first call, it was frankly stated that the experiments were dangerous, and, in case they should be followed by any evil results, in spite of all precautions which the government would take, the inhabitants of that city must not hold the administration responsible. In the other, the attention of volunteers was called to the fact, that, according to estimates, their labors would be required for a term of not less than one year.

Such was the public spirit of those days that half a dozen cities applied at once and fifty thousand veterans, including members of all departments, asked to be enrolled in the service. I was given full charge of the work and I selected from the number of cities that had filed their application, the city of Atlantis, partly because I was more familiar with its system of drainage, and partly because I could count upon the confidence which the inhabitants of that town placed in me. My duties compelled me to remain domiciled in Washington, but as Atlantis could be reached by aeroplane in a few hours, and as such a conveyance was placed at my disposal by the government, I opened a branch office in Atlantis and began my work at once.

To the credit of our veterans, I must say that they worked with a will; ten large reservoirs were built within half a year. An able architect had constructed them in such a manner that the air could be drawn out of them by pumps, so that whenever the drains were opened which connected them with the main pipes, they drew by force of suction the offal which they held into them. Common earth was now mixed with the matter; the chemical compound which I had discovered was infused, and a dough was made of it which a machine pressed automatically into the form of bricks. Whatever foul air arose during the process was led into an electric furnace and consumed by the heat. The bricks had this quality that they would dissolve whenever they were exposed for a couple of weeks to the open air. We sent them to rural districts, where the land had refused to yield fruit. The superintendents of farms were instructed to place them in the furrows, plow them in the spring into the ground, after the winter weather had dissolved them, and then to sow the seed. The expense of the whole process was closely figured and found to be so low that it compared favorably with any of the fertilizers used heretofore.

When the temporary drains were connected for the first time with the mains, and the machinery of my new plant was set to work, the whole country watched in suspense "the marvelous discoveries of Young West," as some called them, or, "the crazy notions of Young West," as my objectors expressed it.

When after a few months, it was found that not an atom of foul air escaped and that the health of the citizens of Atlantis, even of the men employed in the work, had remained unimpaired, I was made the recipient of a grand ovation; the flags of the country were hoisted upon every public building in the city and congratulations poured upon me.

It remained now to be seen whether the land would yield a greater abundance after having been stimulated by my fertilizer. Experments on a very small scale which I had made in previous years on garden patches in the public parks to which I had attended during my leisure hours, had convinced me that my deductions were correct, still I passed through weeks of great mental anxiety. It was indeed not a small matter to me, now that I had succeeded so far, to become the laughing-stock of the country and it required all the encouragement of my friends and especially the reassuring talks of my wife, to keep me in a balanced state of mind.

The reports, however, became more and more hopeful as the season advanced. The weather in general had been fair, though not extraordinarily helpful, but nevertheless, the acres fertilized with our bricks, looked fresher and more promising than the ones to which my composition had not been applied. Every week, I made a trip to these regions to watch the experiment and returned from every one of them inspired with greater hope. At harvest time, the superintendents reported that the fields upon which the experiment had been tried, had yielded three times as much as those that had been managed in the old style.

The problem was solved and as nothing succeeds like success, the country talked for weeks only about "Young West" and his discovery. Every one claimed now that he had known I was right, and that from the beginning, he had prophesied success.

The veterans, who had so cheerfully offered their services, came deservedly in for a great share of the honor; they were now replaced by recruits and regulars and when they were to return home from their extra work, and their companies gathered around the grand stand, at the place where the muster was annually held, they were cheered by the thousands that had come from far and near to witness the remarkable occasion.

In a spirited speech I thanked them for the confidence they had placed in me, holding out their conduct as a shining example to be emulated by future generations.

On the same day a great surprise awaited me. The President, himself, who had come to Atlantis to honor the occasion by his presence, and to render the thanks of the nation to the noble veterans, fastened the blue ribbon to the

button-hole of my coat. He delivered a short
address in which he set forth the duties of good
citizenship and presented me to the people as
one deserving the name of a good citizen. "A
sage of olden times, once said," so he closed,
"that he who makes two blades of grass grow
where formerly but one would flourish, deserves
more praise than the general who killed thousands of people. Mr. West has caused *three*
blades to grow in place of one."

The air was rent by the cheers of the people.
"Young West! Young West!" rolled the cry
from a thousand lips from one end of the place
to the other.

In the cloud of handkerchiefs that were
waved, I beheld only one. As I saw it flutter in
the air, it filled me with greater pride than did
all the combined plaudits of the multitude. It
was the little handkerchief of my wife; it was
Emily who waved it.

CHAPTER VII.

So convincing had been my success, so strik-
ingly had I demonstrated the folly of wasting
the vital forces of the land, that the objectors
to my plans were silenced and the heads of the

departments after a consultation with their
inferior officers, expressed their willingness to
commence at once the work of remodelling the
drainage system of the whole country. To this
I had good reason to object. I had observed
that there was yet much to be improved in the
construction of the plants. I knew that these
improvements could not be accomplished in a
day but that they would suggest themselves as
the work went slowly along, and our experiences
multiplied. If we should go ahead at once on
all points and at the expense of much extra
labor and energy, we would be sure to find a
few years later defects everywhere that would
involve new expense. Success did not blind me
nor was I hot-headed. I proposed to continue
the work slowly, to begin it in the large cities
that were situated on the coast of the Atlantic
and Pacific Oceans, and to work our way by
degrees into the interior. In order not to over-
tax the capacity of the people, I suggested, that
during the next year, only one, the largest and
most populous of our cities, the city of New
York, should be supplied with the new system.
My advice was heeded and I received orders to
commence operations.

I had just begun the preliminary labors of re-
construction, when of a sudden, I had to desist.

Our astronomers had been surprised during the last year by the unforseen appearance of a large and brilliant comet in the eastern sky. Its tail appeared to the naked eye to extend several miles in length and it was at its end one mile, at least, in width. For two months this wondrous star was to be seen every night moving in an angle from east to west until it disappeared in the same inexplicable manner as it had come.

Hundreds of theories were at once set afloat to account for the phenomenon. For several hundred years no comet of such dimensions had been seen, even the one that had appeared in the year 1858, was not to be compared in size with the present one. Simultaneously with these theories, sprang up superstitions of all kinds. Some people believed that the comet was bound to collide either with the moon or with the earth, and that in either case, the end of this globe was near at hand; others, who were less timid, still feared that harm would come to mankind in some other form. "Comets," they said, "have always been forerunners of disasters."

It was in vain that our scientists reminded the people how illogical their fears were and that even in case mishaps should occur they could as little prevent them as they could have prevented the appearance of the star.

Though the science of astronomy had solved many a puzzle, our astronomers did not yet know all. Our professors could give no valid reason in regard to the origin, the peculiar form, the luminous excretion, and the course of the comet; their words, therefore, were received with little credence by the people.

After a while they themselves had cause to become frightened. Various observations indicated to them disturbances that were impending, and, strange to say, whether the comet had anything to do with it or not, the next three years proved to be disastrous.

In Europe and in South America, earthquakes occurred such as had never visited the earth before. A large number of cities in Italy, Greece, Spain, Chili and Brazil were totally destroyed, many lives lost, and hundreds of thousands of people made homeless.

In the interior of Asia, the large rivers suddenly overflowed their banks, covering immense tracts of land with their waters, ruining whole provinces and causing the death of many thousands.

Storms broke out and raged with such a fury on the ocean that the strongest vessels

could not withstand them and went to the
bottom, while the thousands of aeroplanes that
were crossing the air at the time, were carried
to destruction with all their human freight, as if
they had been so many soap-bubbles.

Every day brought news of fresh disasters.
The winter grew extremely severe in the northern and eastern parts of Europe, and, as a con-
sequence, the crops failed in those regions
during the next season, and the people were
threatened with starvation.

All the genius which the human mind could
command, all the courage of which the human
heart was capable was needed to combat these
hostile forces, and had it not been for our
marvelous organization, which was built upon
the solidarity of the whole human race, conditions would have grown more perilous and the
suffering much more intense. As it was, one
nation came to the rescue of another; wherever
damage was done, the industrial armies of the
whole world sent at once men and means to
restore and to build up what had been destroyed. The surplus of one country was used
to cover the deficiencies of another. Never
was the question of indemnification raised;
never was a distinction made between one
nationality and another; never would we call

it charity when we hastened to the rescue of
a sister community. Forming one brotherhood,
we felt duty-bound to stand up manfully for
one another and battle together against the
blind forces of nature, which seemed to have
been set free to annihilate the human race.

It never rains but it pours; to add to the
rest of the misfortunes an epidemic of an unknown nature broke out in the interior of
Africa. Although that continent had been inhabited and had enjoyed a high state of culture
at the time when other continents were yet
covered with primeval forests, it had, nevertheless, remained behind in civilization during the
last millennium, and had not adapted itself as
promptly to the new order of things as had
Europe, Asia, America, or Australia.

The government of that continent was, therefore, slow to discover the threatening danger and
unable, besides, to keep it in bounds. When
the more civilized parts of the world became
aware of it, it was too late to check its progress;
the disease spread all over Europe; from there,
it reached Asia, and it became a mere question
of time when it would visit America. The skill
of the most expert physicians was baffled by it;
medical history showed no precedent from which
to obtain guidance in dealing with it, and no

cause for the disease could be discovered. It would suddenly attack a person, throw him into convulsions, and death would follow after a few hours of intense suffering.

The doctors were nonplussed ; they guessed at medicines, which, however, effected no cure. All that could be done was done to make the sufferers as comfortable as possible in the hours of their agony.

Travel almost entirely ceased ; intercommunication between the nations was practically cut off, excepting the aid which one country brought to another.

Had such evils befallen the inhabitants of this globe during my father's time, when every one cared only for himself, and every member of society stood in a continuous warfare with his next-door neighbor for the support of life, a panic would have broken out ; in the attempt to preserve life, suffering would have been greatly increased, and, panic-stricken, the human hand would have blindly destroyed what the evil forces of nature had left untouched. Only because we stood together in these disastrous days ; only because the feeling of brotherhood united all the inhabitants of the earth, were we able to recover from all these misfortunes with less loss of life and property than would have been the case otherwise.

In spite of all precautions and preventive measures, the epidemic crossed the ocean and reached our country; and what a time we had of it! But we weathered the storm, and the burden borne by all, evenly divided among all, did not crush us as it would have, had we gone into the fight single-handed, every one for himself.

After the epidemic had made the round of the world, it disappeared as suddenly as it had appeared.

Was it to be wondered at, that, under such conditions, all enterprises were dropped that were not urgently demanded by the pressing needs of the moment? Our efforts were to be applied in other directions than to the manufacture of a fertilizer. The administration of President Rust, which had been inaugurated under most promising auspices, was known afterwards as the one in which the most appalling calamities had visited the country, but it was also mentioned as the most self-sacrificing government that ever administrated the land. The members of the cabinet set the example to the rest of the people; all rules as to daily hours of work were suspended; wherever or whenever our presence was needed, we were found in attendance. The chiefs of departments would cheerfully and without murmur take upon themselves the duties that belonged by right to other divisions to relieve their overworked brethren. During the time of the epidemic, for example, we all assisted in reorganizing the hospital service. Inspired by our example, every officer and private in the land gave up his personal convenience, and, without special legislation to that effect, every member of the community not alone increased his daily hours of work but reduced his expenditures so that the common burden should be lessened. " Times will change and must change," they would say, "and when prosperity will smile upon us again, we will have ample opportunities to recuperate."

It is in times of misfortune when the efficiency and the strength of a social order can be tested. During the time of my father's youth, the people stood either in fear of their governments or looked upon them with distrust, even in countries in which the republican form of government was established, because the interests of the governing few and the governed masses were in his time opposed instead of being identical. In our day, people and government are one, their interests are the same; the occupant of the presidential chair and the private, who just entered the ranks of the Industrial Army as a recruit, stand socially and economically on the same level. If a distinction does exist, it is this, that the duties of the former are more onerous than those of the latter, though this is balanced by the honor that is attached to his office.

Thus the people stood by the administration; they never showed the least sign of distrust or dissatisfaction; they had confidence in our foresight and in the experience which we had accumulated during the many years of our services. They also appreciated our devotion to the public cause. As we mourned their losses, so they mourned ours; there was hardly any of us who had not lost a relative or a dear friend.

The epidemic had carried off my mother and my youngest daughter. My mother had reached a ripe old age, and as she would have had to pay her last tribute to nature sooner or later, we mourned not so much that she died, but grieved, having lost in her an excellent friend and an ever-cheerful companion. The loss of our daughter affected us much more, because she was a promising child; but as the country lost in her much more than we did, we would not selfishly single her out from the rest. When we shed tears for her, we bewailed at the same time the loss which the country was suffering in the untimely death of so many young and promising citizens.

At last the tide turned, normal conditions were restored, and the nations of the earth began to remove the traces of the disaster.

By this time I had reached the end, not alone of my official activity, but also of my service in the army. On Muster-day I marched amidst the veterans, and the next day found me a man of leisure.

I had prepared for this event; my experience had shown me that it is less difficult for a person to give up leisure and to enter upon some work than to retire from a life of activity to privacy. It is, after all, work that brings happiness and gives satisfaction, and to be without an occupation is rather a curse than a blessing, especially after years of extraordinary efforts, such as I had passed through.

Previous to my retirement, therefore, I had accepted offices in some of the clubs of which I was a member, and I began now to give my time to them. I also volunteered to take charge of some of the flower beds in the park of the square in which I resided, and more than ever before did I pursue my favorite study, chemistry. Thus my days passed pleasantly by.

My successors in office frequently came to seek my advice, and not only was I delighted to give them the benefit of my long experience, but I never felt irritated or offended when they did not accept my counsel. Many people are sorely hurt when their well-meant advice is not heeded; but how foolish that is! Are our friends not to use their own judgment? Is it not sufficient honor to us that in their search after truth they ask our opinion? If the son should not be wiser than the father, if the successor in an office should not outdo his predecessor, how could the world ever advance? I gave my advice without demanding that it should be heeded. When it coincided with the judgment of the questioner, I felt pleased to observe that my force of mind was yet strong enough to grasp a given situation; if they acted contrary to my counsel, I had often cause to acknowledge that the younger man was clearer in his comprehension of the facts, and in his judgment of their merits, than I was.

I intended to visit other countries, but for two reasons I delayed my project. In the first place, I would not travel unless my wife could accom-

pany me, but she had not yet discharged her
duties to the country, and her time of service did
not expire for three more years. In the second
place, expenditures are increased when one
travels for pleasure, and although our annual
allowance provides for an occasional trip, it is
not by far large enough to cover a prolonged
journey. Our laws, however, permit that
veterans who desire to travel may ask the
government to set aside for their future use the
unexpended amounts of a few terms, which they
will return to the treasury, received from the
time of their application.

My wife, as well as myself, saved, therefore,
during these three years, a sum sufficient to permit us to travel in comfort, and after she had
left the service we took our passports and set
out for a year's trip around the world.

CHAPTER XVIII.

We intended to visit Europe, inspect a part of
Africa, enter Asia from the east, and cross it in
a westerly direction. After reaching the Pacific,
we planned a flying trip to Australia, from there
to Cape Horn, and by land through the length

of the American continent, to return at the expiration of one year.

We had the choice between travel by aeroplane and a sea-voyage. The first was less expensive and would have saved time; however, we chose the second mode of crossing the ocean, partly for the sake of its novelty, partly because one can travel more comfortably by ship than by aeroplane.

Strange to say, ship-building had not been improved in the same proportion as had other branches of architecture. Our ships were still propelled by steam, which was produced by coal-oil instead of coal, and they differed not much from the steamers that crossed the ocean two centuries ago. It is true that our ships are built of aluminum and that the danger of their springing a leak is reduced to a minimum. Between a double wall, the fibers of a plant are pressed, which swell to such an extent when water reaches them that they will stop up any hole or rent which by accident may damage the outward hull of the vessel; otherwise, the form of the vessel, its machinery and its inner arrangements, have remained the same as before.

We make somewhat quicker time; still it takes four days and four nights to reach the nearest European port.

The reasons why so little progress has been made in the art of ship-building are numerous.

On land, electricity can be obtained from our power stations, but on the ocean we have to rely upon steam as the only possible means of propulsion. A great deal of energy has been wasted in former ages in the construction of submarine vessels, but they were of value only when used to destroy the ships of an enemy. Wars ceased when the nations began to understand that the destruction of the property of one country only impoverished the rest; submarine ships are, therefore, of no further use. Why should people travel underneath the water and inhale artificial air when they can much more conveniently skim over the surface of the sea and enjoy the bracing atmosphere of the salt water? The aeroplane which reduced the time in which Europe could be reached by half, had also grown in favor, and owing to that fact no efforts were made to improve the navy. We must not forget, finally, that for more than fifty years, by common agreement, migration had been interdicted. That occurred at the time when the new social order was introduced. Each continent was to work out its destiny and educate the coming generations so as to fit them into the new state of affairs. Ocean travel was,

therefore, greatly reduced, and even the interchange of commodities between one land and
the other was limited. This interruption naturally retarded progress in naval architecture.

We went on board the steamer "Edison,"
named in memory of a renowned electrician of
the nineteenth century, and after an unevent-
ful voyage we arrived on the fourth day in
Brittany. This island was formerly a powerful
country of its own; now it forms simply a
province of Europe. The inhabitants of Brittany were once the masters of the world; they
ruled over a large part of Asia, owned almost
all Australia and a large part of Africa, not to
mention the many islands over which they held
dominion. The new social arrangement which
divided the globe into continents, each standing
under its own government, reduced this part
of Europe to its natural position among the rest.
As it was best equipped for manufacturing purposes, and as its inhabitants were skilled laborers, the land was covered with factories of all
kinds, and most of the commodities which our
country exchanged with Europe are manufactured upon British soil. Since all hostilities
between the European nations had died out, and
rapid and convenient intercommunication had
made near neighbors of them, the European

tribes have intermarried and their various languages have flown into one dialect, which they
speak with more or less purity, as we do the
language of our own country. For international
exchange of thought they use Volapük.

The tourists find many remarkable antiquities
to inspect on this island; the museums of its
cities are stocked to overflowing with relics of
the civilization that preceded ours; otherwise,
life is precisely the same as at home. The
cities are built after the same pattern, the political administration is the same as that developed
by us, and the occupation of the people, as well
as their mode of living, does not materially
differ from ours. The only difference which
I noticed was, that they inclined more towards
manufacture than towards agriculture, and that
the arts were less represented here than I found
them represented in those European provinces
which were formerly known as France, Italy,
and Germany.

London is still an immense city, as large
almost as New York, but neither the luxury
nor the misery for which it was so renowned in
ancient times, and of which the writers of previous ages speak so frequently, is now to be
found there. Every trace of them has been
wiped out. A district of the city, called White

Chapel, which, like the North End of ancient
Boston, had been the resort of the submerged
classes, and hence reeked with filth and squalor,
contains now beautiful squares, in which happy
citizens make happy homes.

Upon my arrival, I reported at once to the
American representative, whom I knew personally very well. He introduced me to the chief
of the exchange department, to whom I had to
deliver the drafts issued by my government,
in order to receive from him an instalment of
expenditure blanks that would pass in all parts
of Europe. We conversed in Volapük, and, to
my annoyance, he addressed me as " Mr. Young
West." Otherwise, I found him a very pleasant host. He introduced me to other members
of the administration, especially to the chief
of the department of sewerage, who begged me
to explain my discoveries and the success which
had so far accompanied my experiments.

By way of the submarine tunnel we reached
the continent, and travelling by rail, aeroplane
and river boats, with an occasional divergence
from the direct route on bicycles, we finally
reached Berlin, the seat of the European administration.

The province of Germany had been first in
the field to discover the principles of our pres-

ent system, and the fermentation had spread
from here. No wonder, therefore, that the
system has reached here its highest perfection.
At least, I observed many arrangements which
I thought might be copied by us to advantage.
The hospital service I found especially superb.
Admirable care is taken to make a patient comfortable and to cure him in as short a time as is
possible. I noticed machines by which the
temperature of a room could be regulated in
such a manner that it corresponded precisely to
the needs of a patient. Also the asylums in
which they keep lunatics were most excellently
managed.

Not that I undervalue our own accomplish-
ments, or that I deprecate the endeavors of our
own officials to do their work well, but I was
forced to acknowledge that the European administration excels ours in precision, for which fact,
however, I found an explanation.

For several centuries the European nations
had accustomed themselves to the strict discipline which the service in their old military
armies prescribed. Their energies, of course,
had then been falsely directed to the destruction
of life and property, but, nevertheless, they had
learned to work together, one for all, and all for
one, at least in this one direction. When they

adopted the truer system and applied military methods to the pursuit of peaceful enterprises, the training which they had received, and which through inheritance had become a part of their nature, made the work easier for them and fitted them better for their new duties. If this hypothesis is not the correct one, I can offer no other, nor can I explain why the service of Europe is carried on in many respects with greater precision than it is in our own country.

While stopping in Berlin, we went one evening to a concert, at which some artists of great renown were to play. I had not carefully read the programme, or the surprise which awaited me upon that occasion would not have been so great. A lady violinist appeared upon the stage. She was a portly woman of my own age; her hair was changing into white, but her eyes were yet full of lustre. A storm of applause greeted her when she entered; she seemed to be a favorite with the audience, and I inquired of a neighbor, who had frantically applauded, who the artist was. " She is an American," said he, " but keep still; she begins to play."

I had heard the same concerto before, but what is more, I had heard it interpreted in the same manner; the same full tones had been drawn from the instrument, which now, as then, seemed to talk, to laugh, to sigh and to weep, only that the musician showed now a still greater mastery of her art.

"That is Violet," I whispered to my wife. We listened with greater interest, and at the same time I scanned carefully her features.

The furrows on her forehead could not have been drawn by time alone; her life, it seemed to me, could not have passed serenely, but what was it that had caused her to age so abnormally? What was it that caused the instrument to betray the troubled heart of the artist.

For many, many years, I had lost sight of her. I had heard that she had married a sculptor, that she had chosen the profession of teacher of music in a conservatory, and that she was sent from time to time to play at concerts in large cities. My love for music, which had grown up so suddenly, had died away as quickly; I had not had time to keep myself posted as in previous years in musical matters. What had been her history?

She had finished, and we joined heartily in the applause which rewarded her and which she so well deserved. Later in the evening, she played another number with the same success, and the audience would not allow her to withdraw until she had given them an encore.

I sent one of the ushers with our cards to her, and received word that she would be pleased to meet us after the concert. Again, I witnessed the honors that were showered upon her by musical critics and enthusiasts in the green room. Now, as in years gone by, she received the homage of her admirers as a matter of course. I introduced my wife to her, and she proposed that we should take lunch together in private at the hotel in which she resided.

Violet had remained the same charming and self-possessed woman that she had been more than thirty years ago. She had passed through many disagreeable experiences, which she did not hesitate to tell us. She had been married four times, and as many times divorced. In vain she had been hunting after an ideal, and as often as she thought she had found a man who fulfilled it, she was disillusioned.

"I should have never married," said she, "because I am too selfish. Accustomed to be worshipped for my art, I demanded to be worshipped in the same manner for my person by my husband. The men I have married never found a companion in me. Indeed it was all my fault. I took never an interest in their work ; I never tried to make them happy,—I lived for my art. When they proposed the severance of an alliance that brought them no happiness, knowing my faults, I acquiesced. I served the country to the best of my ability, and, now that I have retired from the army, I travel lonely from city to city for no other purpose than to play to audiences and to enjoy the tribute that is given to my art. In these regions, I find a greater number of connoisseurs than elsewhere, so I shall stay here quite a while yet."

She was the mother of two children, but as neither of them had inherited any of her talent, she cared little for them ; in fact she did not even know their whereabouts.

My wife felt a great deal of compassion and sympathy for her. "All the love of her art of which she speaks," said she, "is only a pretence, with which she is deceiving herself; it was her misfortune that her first choice of a husband was a mistaken one, and solely because she has never found her true happiness in the companionship of a husband, her life has remained without a mission. The applause of audiences, which she so eagerly seeks, is merely an anæsthetic which she applies to seek forgetfulness. I

pity her with all my soul, and do not envy her
the laurels which she wins."

During our stay in Berlin, we met Violet
frequently; the two women became intimate
friends, and when we parted Violet declared that
she had spent in Emily's company more happy
hours than she had known for years. She
promised to call on us if she ever should return
to America.

The mountainous regions of Europe, especially
the Alps, were delightful; but I had seen similar
landscapes before in my travels across the
American continent. Had it not been for the
people with whom we became acquainted, and
among whom we made many friends, our trip,
as far as seeing novel sights was concerned,
would have been rather uninteresting.

In Italy, we visited the places that had lately
been destroyed by earthquakes. They had been
rebuilt, and but few traces of the calamity were
left. Laborers had been sent by the governments from the remotest parts of Europe to
repair the damage done; the other continents
had sent supplies, and in very short time the
sufferers had been made comfortable again.

We joined a number of tourists in a trip to
Africa. By boat, we passed through the channel that had been built a hundred years ago to

connect the Mediterranean Sea with the interior
of Africa. By means of it, the desolate tract of
land, formerly known as the desert of Sahara,
had been flooded with the waters of the Atlantic, and ships now sail where formerly camels
slowly wended their way. The climatic conditions, not alone of this continent, but also of
the European provinces bordering on the Mediterranean, were so advantageously changed by
this masterpiece of engineering that the outlay
in labor was amply rewarded.

The interior of Africa was still the sore spot
in our civilization. The governments of this
continent had still to fight against atavistic tendencies. There were people yet found among
them, who, without knowing why, would hoard
all kinds of useless articles. Some would quarrel over the possession of certain things, and
instead of applying to a court of arbitration,
they would fall upon each other in a savage
manner. Neither had the women of that continent reached the high standard of culture at
which the women of other countries had arrived; hence, it yet happened that men would
quarrel about the possession of a female who
took their fancy.

Owing to the hot climate, the people of these
regions were not enterprising; only a few of

them had travelled, or were informed in regard to the conditions in which the rest of the nations lived. The masses were yet ignorant of many things.

In conversations with us, some of the more cultured among them inquired what measures we adopted to cure atavism. They wished to know what we did with what they called the criminal classes. They could hardly believe us when we told them that such classes did not exist either in America, Europe, Asia, or Australia and they took notes when we described to them how we eradicated these brutal traits in our nurseries and primary schools by applying the hypnotic process. With high appreciation, they received also the suggestions of a fellow-tourist, who had been a professor of sociology in one of the European colleges.

"In the beginning," said he, "our modern governments had to fight these self-same tendencies of theft and brutality. How did they cure them? Whenever a person was found in whom greed for personal accumulation showed itself, they either loaded him with the care of so much personal property that he grew weary of it, or they employed him to superintend one of their museums. Personal feud they suppressed by putting the guilty party in a cage, exposing him in this condition to the ridicule of the people. After he had promised not to act again like a brute, they transferred him to a distant province where his disgrace was not known, and in every case they found that, after such a treatment, he behaved properly. Women ceased to be the objects of discord after they had learned to take care of themselves, and their favors could no longer be bought by presents."

The African gentlemen, who had listened to these explanations of the professor, doubted whether they could introduce these same methods with effect at once, but promised to try, the professor admitting that such reformations cannot be brought about in a short time, that generations will come and pass before a satisfactory and appreciable change of conditions can be noticed.

Asia had been the cradle of humanity; thus we enlarged our knowledge by studying the remnants of former stages of civilization. We found the people highly interesting. Although their mode of living was like ours in many respects, they seemed to care less for the comforts of life than we do. The youngest among them appeared in their way of thinking to be much older than we were. They had a peculiar way of looking at man's mission on earth, and they gave a great deal of thought to the vexed problem of the origin and the end of all things. Their theories sounded strange to us. They believed that the world, as they saw it, was merely a deceptive vision, a kind of *fata morgana*, and that life was barely worth living. They found their highest consolation in the thought that, after a long process of coming and going, the human soul will finally reach a state of rest, which they called Nirvana. They believed also that after a certain cycle of years the same persons will appear again in life under the same conditions, and act out their existence pre cisely in the same manner in which they had formerly passed through it. These strange theories seemed to enhance their happiness and did not interfere with the working of the social order that had been established everywhere; we found, therefore, no reason to argue the question with them, or to force our beliefs upon them, especially as we are not sure that our theories, explaining the beginning and the end, are any more correct, or help any more to a true solution of the problem.

The year had not yet passed, and we felt already tired of sight-seeing and yearned after a more regulated mode of living than travelling from place to place permits.

We rejoiced when we reached the American continent, fully convinced of the truth of the old saying: " There is no place like home."

CHAPTER XIX.

During the time of my absence, the question had been discussed again whether it was not time to take up the work of reorganizing the sewerage system on the lines which I had proposed many years ago, and demonstrated by successful experiments to be not alone urgent but feasible.

Opponents had been silenced in so far as the practicability of the enterprise was concerned, but the years of misfortune through which we had passed had taxed so much the working capacity of the nation that objectors claimed, people were not prepared at present to enter upon a work of such magnitude. The artisans, manufacturers, machinists, electricians and architects claimed that with the new enterprise on hand their daily hours of work could not be lessened, but were likely to be increased. The agriculturists, on the other hand, demonstrated that unless they gave longer hours to their work they would not be able to supply the increasing wants of an increasing population from a soil that had gradually become exhausted. Some. departments were, therefore, in favor of taking up the work where I had dropped it on account of the disastrous years; others insisted that the people required a rest for a number of years, and that no new work should be taken up for quite a while.

The time for the election of a new president had arrived. If I desired ever to reach the goal of my ambition, this was the time, because only in rare cases were the people inclined to elect to the presidency a man who was older than fifty-five or fifty-six years, or who had been retired from the public service for more than five years. If, however, I intended to offer myself as a candidate, the battle had to be fought on the ground of the principle before mentioned.

Many of my friends encouraged me to seek the office. Robert Dudley, one of my oldest friends, was particularly urgent, and impetuously brought my name before the conventions of various of the guilds. The reader will, perhaps, recognize in him my playmate in the nursery, known then as Bobby — the very one who was solely responsible for the nickname "Young West," which since that time has so persistently clung to me.

His career, too, had been a remarkable one.
His natural inclinations had made him useful in
the large slaughter houses of the nation, and he
had chosen that occupation. He rose from
office to office until he finally became head of
the section which took charge of the meat
supply of the whole country. During the time
when I served in the cabinet, he, too, was a
member of it, leaving, however, both this
honored position and the army one year before
me. His connection with the various guilds of
the agricultural department made him a valuable advocate for my nomination.

The nominating conventions proposed, therefore, to the choice of the people, my name and
that of a former member of the electrical department.

Mr. Blank, my rival, was a very deserving
man, who had enriched the country by various
valuable inventions. Like myself, he had
been honored with the blue ribbon. He was a
personal friend of mine; he had been in the cabinet with me, and we had worked faithfully
together during the trying years of the epidemic.
Personally, of course, we had no fault to find
with each other; we disagreed only on the
principles in question. His friends and supporters were as numerous as were mine, and

when the nomination was announced, the knowing ones predicted that whoever of us would be
elected would become president only by a small
majority.

We both began now to travel and to address
the voters in order to explain to them the real
issue upon which their votes were solicited.
We often appeared together before an audience,
and, as there were no personalities in the campaign, we having no cause whatsoever to belittle
each others merits, these discussions and debates
tended to bring our differences more accurately
before the people.

Mr. Blank was the better orator; his training
had developed his gift of speech, and not unfrequently would he carry an audience by storm.
I could win the favor of my hearers only by the
better arguments. I stated the unreasonable-
ness of wasting the earth's vitality when we
could apply it to improve not only our own conditions but those of the generations that are to
follow; I showed how the work, once completed,
would save labor and that all fear of a famine or
even scarcity would be forever banished. How
could we perform the necessary work of the
social body well unless we were all well fed?
How could we produce a sufficient supply if we
did not return to mother earth what we yearly

draw from her? I admitted that for a number
of years an additional expenditure of labor
would be demanded, but, after that, so much
less would be asked of the people.

Perhaps it was the sounder argument that I
offered; perhaps it was my appeal to the indus-
trious habits of the people which brought me
their votes; still, I cannot help suspecting that
my name was a great help to me. The nickname, " Young West," which had so frequently
irritated me, and which, to hear, caused me
even pain in this campaign, had become a catch-
word that took with the people. We hardly
imagined what a power a catch-word is to move
the sympathies and imaginations of the masses
of men. The rallying cry was " Young West
against Mr. Blank," and this very adjective
" Young," though it was not appropriately connected with my name, carried the day. The
appellation took the fancy of the voters. But
the widest divergencies of opinion as to the
merits of the proposed change obtained among
the sections of the various departments, and
even among the members of a section, so that
the wisest would not risk any prophecy as to the
outcome of the election.

The days previous to election day were days
of great mental strain to me. Not that I feared

a great harm would come to the country
if I should fail; not that I had any personal
advantages to expect; quite to the contrary, I
knew that my capacity for work would be taxed
to the utmost; but I was human. To seek the
honor of an office, even if we have to pay for it
by the increased work connected with it, was
one of the aspirations which our system of
training inculcates into the mind of every child.
I had striven for this honor for many, many
years, particularly since I was married. My
wife had always kept these ambitious desires
ablaze, and now failure would have brought me
a touch of humiliation. How selfish I was! I
thought little of how humiliation would affect
my rival; during these days of excitement and
anxiety I confess I thought only of myself.

At last the hour of decision came; reports
began to arrive from all parts of the country —
some favorable, some discouraging. Then the
news came that votes were cast for me in a
sufficient number of departments to assure my
election. Finally, the official telegram announced the official count; the figures showed
that " Young West " had been elected president
by a large majority.

I heard the people cheering in the streets;
my friends filled the parlors of the house in

which I resided, ready to shake hands with the president-elect; my wife shed tears of delight in my arms; my children and my nearest relatives, who had come to be with me on this auspicious day, brought me their congratulations. It was a moment of exaltation, of supreme emotion; and in the midst of my honor and triumph came into my mind the depressing thought that defeat had humiliated my friend Blank in the same degree as success had elevated me.

Through a side-entrance I slipped out of the house and sought him, asking his forgiveness if my success should have caused him pain, and begging him to help me accomplish the mission for which the people had evidently chosen me.

He met me with the same generous and manly spirit he had always exhibited in every stage of his career. Now that all was over, he was ready to yield to the public will; he promised to exert whatever influence he possessed in my behalf, and to help me in the coming work to the best of his ability.

I took him with me to my house, and the crowds that filed by to congratulate me on the occasion saw us together. They shook hands with him, as they did with me; they cheered us both lustily. I felt doubly happy, because I had won him to share in the triumph.

On the day appointed for the ceremony, I was inaugurated into the office, and inasmuch as my election meant the speedy performance of a proposed work, I began it at once.

Policy had not dictated my conduct toward Mr. Blank. It had been entirely the result of a strong momentary emotion, but it won for me the hearts of the people.

Blank himself became now a most eloquent advocate of my plans. "I opposed 'Young West,'" said he, "because I thought you weary and worn out by the additional work which the disastrous years had imposed upon you. I was evidently mistaken, since you feel yourselves strong, you show willingness to undertake an enterprise of so great dimensions, I say, very well, fulfill your pledges."

I issued a call for volunteers, and the veterans of all guilds and of all provinces responded at once. So eager were they to complete the work, that, not unfrequently, I had to put on the brakes lest they would do harm to themselves.

Before two years had passed, the oceans were fed no longer with the vitals of the earth; what was taken from the land was returned to it after

it had served to support human-life.   At the
expiration of my term, the transformation of
the sewerage system of the land was completed.
The country bloomed like a garden, it yielded
fruit in abundance, and the people blessed me
for it.

Other nations sent their delegates to examine
our system in order to copy it, which, of course
increased the love and the respect my fellow-
citizens extended to me.

The years of my administration were also
otherwise prosperous.   No disasters of any kind
befell the community; crops were plentiful; the
people were contented, and had it not been for
the extra work which the construction of my
new system of sewerage demanded, my labors
during the presidential term would have been
only nominal.   Like a well-oiled machine, society moved without friction during these years,
so that it could be truthfully said that the
presidential administration of "Young West"
was one of the most successful ever recorded in
the annals of the country.

I had now served my fellow-citizens many
years.   Thirty years in the army, and, after a
lapse of five years, as president for five years.
Having reached my sixty first year, I now retired for good, but as it was customary that

every ex-president should make himself useful to the country for five more years as a member of the World's Court of Arbitration, I remained still on deck.   The duties of that office were not onerous, though they were of high importance.

The ex-presidents of the five continents formed a Court of Arbitration.   Whenever two governments happened to come into a conflict which they could not amicably settle between themselves, they brought their grievances before this court.   Their representatives in the court would then assume the parts of plaintiff and defendant, and their three colleagues the position of judges.   If, for example, differences arose between Europe and Asia, the ex-presidents of these continents placed the matter before the tribunal, and the ex-presidents of America, Africa and Australia, after having heard all the evidence, passed judgment, which in all cases was to be heeded.

During the five years in which I served in that capacity, this court was convened only twice: once in a conflict between Asia and Africa; another time in a suit which our government brought against the administration of Europe.   In both cases the difficulties were satisfactorily settled.

I looked forward upon my approaching old

age with joy. My life's work was done and I was yet able to be thrilled by many pleasure-giving sensations. My children filled honorable positions in the army, according to their talents and tastes. I could not expect that they should reach the same prominence in public affairs that my good fortune had secured for me; as long as they were happy in their chosen professions, why should their lack of ambition trouble me?

I laid out my plans how to divide my time between study and recreation. As I still loved physical exercises, I decided to leave Washington and to retire to Denver, in the neighborhood of which city I had spent four pleasant years when I was at high school. I selected that city partly because the farms in which I had worked when a boy offered me a chance to exercise my body in a pleasant manner; partly because my sister Edith lived in retirement in the same place.

I had not seen her for many years. The last time we had met was at the cremation of my mother, but as this happened during the calamitous year of the epidemic, when, on account of the high rate of mortality, these ceremonials were cut short, we had barely time to converse for a few moments. She had to return to

the hospital, in which her presence as physician
was needed; I had to return to my duties
as cabinet officer, which, at that trying time,
demanded my whole strength and attention.

My wife was satisfied with my arrangements,
and we prepared to go westward.

We had lived in the capital for the last
twenty years, and counted friends there by the
hundreds. Before leaving they showed us
their good will, as had our fellow-citizens of
Atlantis. The largest hall in the city hardly
held the crowds of friends who came to shake
hands with us, and the orations which were
made on the occasion, and which set forth the
esteem and love which the assembled guests
bore us, appeared to me like the eulogies in
a crematory, with the only difference that the
eulogized person was alive and heard them. If
there exists any true reward for faithful services
rendered to the community, it is the appreciation of the ones who are benefited by them.
People will give their best work during a whole
lifetime, in order that their efforts should be
praised by their surviving friends after death,
though they themselves cannot hear what is
said about them. I had the satisfaction of
receiving the expressions of approval on the
part of friends, none of whom could ever expect

any personal benefits from me. Had they not felt sincerely what they said, nothing would have induced them to say it.

Still larger were the crowds of people that surrounded the aeroplane station when we departed. As on the occasion when I received the blue ribbon, handkerchiefs were waved as we rose in the air, and from the distance, came to us the shout: " Farewell to YOUNG WEST! YOUNG WEST! West!"

Emily was sitting on deck by my side, resting her head on my shoulder. I whispered into her ear: "All this happiness I owe to you; they ought to cheer you, not me." She answered: "Let it rather be as it is; I feel so proud, so proud of you."

CHAPTER XX.

After we had been comfortably settled in our new home, and had begun the routine of our new life, we called one day on my sister. We found her busy arranging some of her papers, and, as it happened, she just laid aside a book which seemed familiar to me. I remembered having seen it before. It was the volume of recipes which my mother had taken from her father's library as a keepsake after his death. Edith told me, I was right; that by way of bequest it had come to her and that it had served her to good purpose many a time.

"This reminds me," said she, looking up from her work of assorting papers, "I have in my possession something that will surely interest you. You know mother died in my arms; she was nursed in the hospital, in which then I served as head physician. After her cremation I returned her personal property to the stock- rooms, keeping only her papers. For many years I left them untouched, with the exception of grandfather's recipes. Once, however, when I assorted them in an hour of leisure, as you see me now going through these papers, a bundle of letters fell into my hands, which I opened and found to be epistles which your father had directed to mother when he was absent on lec- ture trips. I read one or two of them, but, as they had little interest for me, I put them aside, intending to give them to you when- ever we should next meet. The matter, after a while, escaped my memory, and had you not by chance remembered having seen the recipes, I might never have thought of it. Here are the letters. Perhaps they will interest you." Saying this, she handed me a bundle of papers, yellow with age.

My curiosity was indeed aroused. My father's life was so much bound up with mine, and the lectures which he once delivered, and which I kept in my possession as a sacred heirloom, had so frequently given me food for thought that I valued every scrap of manuscript coming from him. That very evening I sat down with my wife to read these epistles.

We both were disappointed; they were quaint in style and abounded in sentiments which we could scarcely comprehend. Father apparently looked upon his wife as upon a person who could not well take care of herself, and over whom he was set to keep watch. Some passages contained superficial flatteries, by which the writer evidently intended to humor his correspondent. Whenever he described sights that were new to him, and reflected upon them, he showed unmistakably that he did not fully understand the subjects about which he was writing.

We were about to stop reading that evening, and to postpone the perusal of the rest of the letters to some other evening, when we came upon an envelope which was not addressed to my mother, but which bore the somewhat ominous superscription: "Confessions." We opened it and our curiosity grew, when, besides a package of papers written in his hand, a slip, written by mother, fell from it. My wife picked it from the floor, to which it had fallen, and read:

"I found these papers after the death of my beloved husband; I intended to burn them, but a second sober thought convinced me that they might be of value to posterity. Love, pity, and reverence persuaded me not to make public these pages during my lifetime, and rather to leave it to chance to bring them to the notice of people. May the good judgment of the ones into whose possession these papers may fall decide what to do with them.

EDITH LEETE WEST.

We quickly opened the manuscript, and, to our great surprise, we read as follows:

"My days are numbered; I feel my life fast ebbing away, but I am not afraid to die. Quite to the contrary, I look forward to the final dissolution with gladness. Why? Have I drained the pleasures of life to the last drop so that nothing remains in the cup but the bitter dregs? Or do I suffer pain or privation? By no means. I am weary of life because strange circumstances prevent me from being true to myself and true to others."

" I call it now a misfortune that I was restored to life after a sleep of more than a hundred years. Oh, that this sleep would never
have been interrupted! O! that I had died
rather than have been resuscitated! I suffer
unspeakably because I suffer in silence, because
there is nobody whom I could invite into my
confidence. There are none who could understand me. Not even my faithful wife knows
how miserable I am, and if she knew, I doubt
whether she could sympathize with me. I
write these lines in the silence of the night,
seeking relief by thus unburdening my troubled
soul."

" When I awoke from my protracted slumber
I found myself in a world so different from the
one in which I had lived before that I am often
in doubt whether all is not a dream. So different are all the conditions and social arrangements that surround me from those to which
my early education and training had accustomed
me, that I am thrown in constant conflict with myself. I cannot deny that during my sleep the
world has wonderfully progressed; I found a
haven of peace in place of a battlefield; I found
a loving and lovable brotherhood where I had left
individuals fighting with individuals for a crumb
of bread; I found cleanliness where I had left
squalor: order where I had left confusion. I
was received not as a stranger who had no right
to a living, but with love and tolerance. My
wants were liberally supplied, and that the
faintest feeling of dependency should be re-

moved, I was given employment suitable to my abilities. I found a loving wife, and if death will but delay his approach I may revel even in joys of fatherhood. How can I, therefore, express openly dissatisfaction with existing conditions? Would it not be ungrateful on my part were I to censure a social order from which I derive so many benefactions? Would people, after all, understand me? Could they place themselves in my position?"

"But, alas, my lips sing praises to which my heart does not respond. I am morally compelled to acknowledge the present social order as perfect, and yet my soul rebels against it. Does all this not sound like the raving of a lunatic? Reader, do not think that I am demented. I am sound in mind; I feel what I say and say what I feel."

"With all its advantages over my previous life, my present existence does not satisfy me. I miss too many conditions that were dear to me by force of habit. The very absence of worry, of care, oppresses me like a calm on the ocean oppresses the sailor. I do not live — I vegetate. Not alone that it is easy to be good, not alone that virtue has ceased to be the result of strife, it is difficult, nay, impossible, to go wrong. What glory, therefore, in goodness? I miss the shadow that relieves the dazzling light of virtue. Moreover, in whatever relation I am placed to others, I find myself the diminutive, insignificant part of a whole. After I have done my best, I am no more than is my neighbor, who also has done his best according to his abilities. There are no distinguishing lines between man and man: I am placed on a dead level with the rest; I am lost in the crowd."

"How pleasant it was to hope for and believe in a reward for virtue and in a punishment for wrong-doing! How soothing was the expectation that the one who suffered on earth would rejoice in another existence after death, while those who rejoiced here would be laid low there. I am robbed of this hope, of this belief, of this expectation, because suffering on this earth has been reduced and wrong-doing has been eliminated. No future can be imagined by the human mind that would be much improvement on the present."

"Most all of man's personal responsibilities have been taken from his shoulders, except the one inclusive responsibility of serving the commonwealth to the best of his abilities. The parent is no longer responsible for the proper bringing up of his offspring; the husband is not held to protect his wife, neither is the child asked to assist the originators of his existence in their declining age. Wherever I turn, I confront the self-same spectral, abstract idea of the commonwealth. The commonwealth is the parent, the commonwealth is the child, the commonwealth is the God, who carries all and is worshipped by all."

"True, that religion is no longer needed to curb the passions of man, to inspire him to noble deeds; true. that the very ideals of religion have taken shape and have entered life as realities, and yet how I miss the sweet consolation and the inspiration that came to me in my early days through religious worship. At that time, I could pray. Even if I did not expect that my prayers should be answered, they were at least the expression of my hopes for something better; but how can I pray for the better when I possess the best possible on earth?"

"How sweet it was to be charitable! What a pleasure it was to give of my affluence to others; what satisfaction I derived when I dried a tear and received the grateful look of a person whom I helped out of his difficulties! Now, nobody needs my aid; I neither give nor receive presents! Economic equality has made all free, but has it not at the same time destroyed some of the love that springs from our dependence upon others, from the acknowledgment of our weakness? Can I love the child that grows up in independence far from me, and upon whom I never expect to depend? Can I love the wife whom I do not support and protect? Can I love a brother or sister in blood with whom I come in contact but occasionally, and who stands not nearer to me than the thousands of others with whom, and for whom, I am expected to work?"

"I own, I am stirred by passions. I wish to possess, and to possess things for my own sole benefit. The thought alone that a thing is *mine* makes it valuable to me, makes me care for it.

If I give away to others of what I own, I want
to receive as a reward the pleasures which charity includes.   I want the house in which I live,
were it but small, to be *mine ;* the wife of my
bosom to be unreservedly *mine ;* the child I
issue to be *mine ;* the field I work in to be *mine ;*
I want to be free to give what I own to whom I
please."

"I will admit that the social order in which I
was brought up had its evils.   After having
seen the present state of society, I could never
return and live happy in the former.   I will
even confess that a dream which once brought
me back to it was a horror to me and made me
miserable for days ; but, nevertheless, I feel that
I have bought the happiness of the present at
too high a price.

"I yearn for death because I am not fit to
live in the present age on account of my early
education, and unfit to live again in the past on
account of the lessons which the present has
taught me.   This discord is worse than death.
Were I to praise the past at the expense of the
present, were I to express a wish for the reëstab-
lishment of the former social order, I would be
untrue; so am I untrue when I extol the
present.   It is well for me to die." —— ——

The letter bore my father's signature and
was dated one month before his death.   Having
read this strange paper, I folded it and we
looked at one another in silent astonishment.
At last Emily began :

"Poor father West, how I pity you. I do understand you ; therefore my heart goes out to you and throbs in sympathy for you. What an agony, what a torment life must have been to you ! "

I nodded assent. " Indeed," said I, " under the conditions it was far better for him to die than to live. There was no remedy for his ills. It was not the fault of society that caused his melancholy feelings, it was his early education that unfitted him for this life. He had imbibed the ideas and principles upon which the social order of his day was founded; they had, so to say, been burned into his soul ; how could he have torn them out of his heart without lacerating it ? Alas, we move not in leaps and bounds. The transformation of conditions progresses too slowly to be observed, so that after a change has become noticeable the creatures of a former stage have become unfit to live in the new world. We cannot jump into a new social order, but must grow into it. I am sure that we could not live happily in the time to come, say, one hundred years from now, after society will again have changed its forms. Wise and beneficient is nature, therefore, that it removes us from the stage when a new play, for which we have not rehearsed, is to be enacted. The wish to live

in a future age, or to have lived in the past, considers not our fitness, or rather unfitness, to
accomodate ourselves to a different order of
things from that in which we were raised. The
present only is ours ; to the present we belong ;
with the present let us die."

"You are right," said Emily, "no matter how
glorious conditions, that are to come, may appear to be, we could never enjoy them unless
we had grown into them. Your father's confession makes me think of his many contemporaries, who, as we know, dreamed in the turmoil of their time of an order of society similar
to ours. Suffering from the evils that sprang
from the competitive strife in which they were
engaged, they wished for conditions like ours,
they wished for economic equality, for a time
of peace and universal happiness, resulting from
the recognition of every person's right to life,
and the enjoyment of life. If they could have
realized their wishes of a sudden ; if, like your
father, they could have passed the period of
transition in sleep and that kingdom of heaven,
the establishment and realization of economic
equality would have suddenly fallen upon them,
they would have become as dissatisfied and
melancholy as has your father, simply because
they were not ready to pay the price for these

new institutions, simply because they would not or could not have put away the ideas, associations, customs and views of life under which they had been reared."

"Shall I publish this letter," asked I?

"I think it best to tear up the manuscript," replied Emily, "because its publication would destroy the reverence and the respect in which your father's memory is held among us. Were it not for that consideration, I would advise to publish it, in order to warn some of our own contemporaries who, like your father and the people of his time, hope so much from the future, never to expect that they themselves could ever live happy in a commonwealth as they construct it in their thoughts. They might learn from your father's sad experience that the social reformer must be unselfishness personified. He must never expect to derive any benefit for himself; he must never hope to enter himself the land into which he is leading others; he must never try to hasten the natural and rational development of conditions. He may show the way; he may prophesy what will happen; he may argue the justice of a measure, or denounce the injustice of an established law; he may prepare the minds of people for the coming change, but beyond that he must not go."

We cut the paper into small pieces, opened the window, and in small portions we allowed the wind to carry over hill and dale the confessions of Julian West, senior.

* * * * * * * *

I have no fault to find with my conditions. Though I am approaching the end of my life, there is sunshine behind me, light before me. When the hour of departure will strike, I will die satisfied that I have enjoyed every moment of life, and that I have given an equivalent for every enjoyment by faithful work. I feel grateful that I was permitted to pass my existence now, and not in my father's time, and although my faith is firm that mankind will advance and reach a still higher plane of culture, I do not yearn to live in that future time.

The experiences of my life are the experiences of all the members of the present social order, in a general way; they may vary in color, but they do not vary in kind. We are forming one happy family. Indeed:

" This world is full of beauty, as other worlds above;
    Because we do our duty, it is as full of love."

THE END.